The Beautiful Side of Submission

Authority and Submission in Balance

Lela Johnson

The Beautiful Side of Submission: Authority and Submission in Balance
by Lela Johnson
ISBN: 0-88270-688-8
Library of Congress Catalog Card Number: 95-83027
Copyright © 1996 by **BRIDGE-LOGOS** *Publishers*

Published by:
BRIDGE-LOGOS *Publishers*
North Brunswick Corportate Center
1300 Airport Drive, Suite E
North Brunswick, NJ 08902

Table of Contents

Dedication

This book is dedicated to my husband, David, who was a living demonstration of the true meaning of the beautiful side of submission.

Acknowledgments

A special thanks to Jeanette (Klippel) Crawford for her patience and persistence during the many hours of typing as she performed the tedious task of putting the manuscript on computer in its early stages—and for her artistic talent. Also to Holly Wilson, the editor whom the Lord sent at just the right time to help make the manuscript acceptable. And thanks to Nadia Doran and Jeane Mulreany for their input— and to my son, Bryan, for lending his wisdom and help with the computer, which was so foreign to me. Also thanks to my daughter, Heather, whose love and encouragement helped keep me going.

A host of other people, some who were old friends and some who became new ones, gave me invaluable help, encouragement, and insight—and encouraged me to persevere during the years this book was being written. My thanks to each of them, and to those who so generously allowed their stories to be recorded here. Space constraints prevent me from naming them all, but my heartfelt thanks to each—I couldn't have done it without you.

Last, but not least, my appreciation and thanks to my family for their patience and willingness to be identified. God bless you. If there are eternal rewards they will be shared by all.

Preface

While much of the erroneous and harmful teaching on submission has, with the passage of time, diffused itself through the Christian community, its residual negative effect is still apparent to the discerning heart. Subtle but crippling scars remain. However, the truth of the submission principle is still needed today because it's the way God has for us to show His kind of love to each other in all of our relationships, especially family and church where the warp and woof of life is lived out.

As a wife of almost 34 years and now a widow, a mother of two and a grandmother, with a daughter in college and a son in the ministry, I've lived out many of the problems that are touched on in this book as they relate to family and church. I began my working life in a business office. Then I returned to my first love, piano teaching, and have continued with that these many years. The combination gave me valuable experience in the business and professional world as well as home and church.

I've been a Christian since I was 21, and committed to personal study and application of God's Word in my own life. Much of the message within these pages I've discovered from experience, searching for answers, and proving the biblical principles through routine living. I've served in many capacities within the local church and in recent years received a Ministerial Arts Degree from Trinity School of the Bible. I'm now ordained as a Pastoral Counselor.

Through it all, I've continued to feel there is a need for the message contained in these pages. This book is not intended to read like a novel—it is rather for study and contemplation. Of necessity, it's presented in broad principles because of the variety of circumstances the readers will bring to it. For this reason, surface perusal will not do. I don't presume to have all the answers, but it's my hope that the thoughts presented here will shed some light on the pathway of other pilgrims who follow where I've been.

I've attempted to present the subject of submission from the viewpoint of one who's not in authority but with an appreciation for the position of those who are. I'm speaking on behalf of the many who desire to see that those who hold authoritative responsibility be given a fuller understanding of the impact their attitudes and actions have on those who serve under them. In a word: *accountability*.

There's a need for significance in everyone and most of us desire to fit into God's plan, but many haven't been able to find a place of usefulness within the context of the local church—others have never been challenged to do so. Understanding God's plan for relationships is vital as He brings end-time changes to His Church.

So I've written this book from the viewpoint of the Christian layman—that of a sheep seeking a right relationship with the true Shepherd, Jesus Christ. And then, having found that relationship, seeking a right relationship with the undershepherds and the rest of the flock. The key resource and guide for such relationships is the Bible.

Since submission is primary to biblical relationships, this book is for people who need clarification as to how it applies to their lives. The principles advocated here have been hammered out on the anvil of experience, some good and some not so good, but all instructive. Some are my own struggle—but most have come to me through my experiences as a lay counselor and trying to understand and explain to others the Church and Christian life today as contrasted to that which we see in the early Church and in the life and teachings of our Lord.

The goal of this book is to bring understanding and healing to the victims of wrong concepts concerning these things. Often I have not been able to guide people past the pitfalls of faulty teaching on submission and have seen the devastating results; therefore, my studies of the subject have compelled me to write this book.

The *Beautiful Side Of Submission* is about relationships that result in harmony and peace with God and our fellowmen. These can be ours when we follow the pathway of submission and authority that God has given, without losing the individuality He also intends us to have.

Beautiful relationships are possible when they're based on love expressed through submission one to another in a context of responsibility and accountability.

Lela Johnson
Brookings, Oregon
1995

1

Submission With Freedom

God's Plan

Loving relationships with other people are the only things of earth we take with us when we enter eternity. For that reason they're part of our purpose on earth and should be valued above all else. Because they're so important, God has given us a plan for successfully handling every aspect of the relationships we encounter. Submission is a significant part of that plan. Does that surprise you? It does most people.

God's plan is for a relationship in which there is joy and freedom because of the love that surrounds it. Contrary to popular opinion, from God's perspective, submission isn't a bad word. It's not another word for submersion, subjugation or bondage. Instead, under the proper conditions, it's a beautiful expression of genuine love. Submission freely given to responsible and accountable authority is our Creator's plan for order and harmony.

God's system of authority is patterned after His Kingdom where the angels give unwavering obedience to

His every command. His authority on earth is no less real. But on earth He chose to limit Himself to exercising that authority through human beings. So He gave them dominion over every other living creature.

Man's spirit was created in the image of God, but his body was formed out of the dust of the ground (Genesis 2:7). Although the human spirit wasn't included in the realm of man's domination, there is one spirit that man *is* to dominate—his own. Proverbs 16:32 tells us that man is to rule his own spirit, taking responsibility for his attitudes and actions. Accordingly, the Holy Spirit helps us submit through the fruit of self control. Please note that although the Holy Spirit is God, He doesn't control us—He helps us to control ourselves.

The Effect of The Fall

When Adam and Eve disobeyed God, they were spiritually separated from Him and could no longer communicate with Him. So God instituted blood sacrifices as the only means by which men and women with their new sin nature could approach Him. He also began to use circumstances and suffering as a means by which to open their will to Him and bring it in line with His own.

As men and women succumbed to the effects of sin, their fallen nature quickly trapped them in the very relationship problems from which God's plan was designed to protect them. Genesis 1:28 says that God gave dominion to both the man and the woman. From the first they were treated as equal partners whom God had made different to complete each other.

God gave the man the place of initiator, of provider and protector, and gave him attributes for headship. He gave

2

the woman attributes that complimented and completed the man—a helper equipped to meet his needs. As it's written in Genesis 2:20, a "suitable helper" for him, meaning one who was comparable to him. Both are necessary to make a complete unit, but each one also stands before God as an individual.

Masculine strength was intended for leadership, feminine softness for comfort and nurture. Because of their fallen nature, however, men's strength was soon perverted into domination of women (possibly as subconscious revenge for the woman's part in the fall). From there, men's desire for dominion over others led to strife and war that has continued throughout history.

Although wars will continue unto the end of the earth, the status of women was restored by Jesus so that once again we can celebrate the differences between the sexes without touting the superiority of either. He honored the place of women as no other man before Him had done, and left a legacy of equality for us—yet, at the same time, God's Word teaches submission. Submission is not a put-down for women, however, it's simply the way spiritual reality works, a governing principle instituted by God for the harmony of His kingdom.

Government Begins

God began human government after the flood by establishing a covenant with Noah as head of the family from which the whole earth would be populated (Genesis 9:19). Noah was given responsibility for earthly welfare and punishment and a pattern for continuing accountability to God (Genesis 9:1-6). His first act after leaving the ark was to worship God with a sacrifice of clean animals and birds. He was then commanded to repopulate the earth, and given the rainbow as a sign of God's covenant promise to him (Genesis 9:12-17). As Noah continued to find grace in the eyes of the Lord, his descendants grew into the hundreds and spread throughout the known earth.

Without respect for Noah's God-given authority, that first government—the family—would never have succeeded—it would have degenerated into warring fractions. Respect for authority must still begin with the family, and then extend to society as a whole through the government and the Church.

The Place of Respect

Respect is a precursor of submission. We owe appropriate respect to others, beginning with parents, spouses, and children. We owe respect to those in places of authority, in government, and the workplace. Respect is also due to those whom the Lord commands us to serve in love, but this respect must be based upon recognition of our equality, or that love has a hollow ring.

Respectful service matures into submission when the act of submission becomes a willing sacrifice. If service is motivated by undue control, however, it is not submission but subjugation, which is not what Christ taught or intends for those in His Church.

As Christians, the Holy Spirit works in us to put Kingdom principles of equality in our hearts. Paul's admonition to submit to one another is the cure for the sin of domination (or control) in the Church. Submission of wives to the leadership of husbands and husbands submitting to the responsibility of leadership *under Christ* are the keys to allowing God to deal with the sin of excessive control in the family.

Submission cannot be demanded from another person, however, any more than you can demand love. When you're freely living in submission, you've *chosen* to live by principles of love—and choice means freedom. Through submission, God has given us a practical way to express love in our attitudes and actions, a way which authenticates the words, "I love you."

The World We Live In

Since the concept of loving submission is based on a loving and obedient relationship with God, it's understandable that society as a whole fails to grasp its truth. For the first two hundred years of American history the Church was salt and light to the world and formed the basis for society's moral values. Healthy submission was then taken for granted. During that time our culture was based on its Christian roots and the Bible was taught and accepted as truth and moral guide.

Although God's blessing has been on this land since its inception, this century has seen the erosion of living by Biblical principles. What began as an amoral trickle in our society has become an avalanche. The effect has been the breakdown of Christian influence on every level. As Christian influence diminished to an all-time low, so did respect, responsibility, and commitment—those things that are essential to loving submission.

How Submission Went Wrong

In 1946, Dr. Benjamin Leland Spock, a pediatrician/psychiatrist, wrote a book—*The Commonsense Book of Baby and Child Care*—which revolutionized the way most parents raised their children. The book brought in an era of permissive parenting, and by the sixties and seventies many of the young people of the 'Spock generation' were in open rebellion to any form of authority. Their resulting destructive behavior was of major concern as many college campuses erupted into violence and became havens of a rising drug culture. The revolution of low-to-no moral values and standards that they started has since torn our nation's education and politics away from its Christian foundation.

Because a whole generation of our brightest young people were in the forefront with rebellious attitudes, permissive parents and adults often gave credence to their views and actions. As a result, the ugly tentacles of an amoral cultural revolution spread unchecked throughout society. A quarter century later, many who instigated or were part of the revolution have now gained respectability and power through their adult activities, especially in such fields as entertainment, business, politics, and even religion.

The rejection of established moral values exposed a spiritual vacuum to which the Church responded slowly, if at all. Because of the crazy world they inherited—and helped to create, many of the young people were adrift and searching for reality, mostly in the wrong places. In an attempt to find meaning to life, some indulged themselves in sexual freedom, some gravitated toward eastern philosophy, and many experimented with drugs.

That generation of hippies and flower children had a valid reason to speak out about the society in which they found themselves. The liberties that they declared to be their rights, however, soon tragically became their bondage. But it was while they were in that bondage that many were exposed to the truth of the Gospel of Jesus Christ, and their spiritual poverty became an open door that they walked through to salvation. The Lord brought in a mighty harvest of souls, and the Jesus movement was launched. Some great Christian churches were birthed in that time and are still strong.

When these young people became Christians they brought with them a life style of independence and a questioning search for truth. Disciplining them was a challenge to church leaders since that youth culture was from a whole new kind of world. Because of their outward appearance they were sometimes rejected by traditional churches, so new ministries were formed that were more in line with their culture and spiritual needs.

Since a concept of submission to authority seemed to be a major ingredient missing in their culture, its emphasis became the counteracting force designed to restore what had been lost. Order and control had to be re-established and so, in some Christian circles, there sprang up a teaching of God's order of submission as the spiritual leaders understood it.

Unfortunately, as with almost all new religious movements, an extreme form of submission quickly developed. The extreme was in teaching that God demands absolute submission *without question* to authority that has been placed over us in the Church. It was as though Church authority speaks as God Himself. The harm in that early form of submission was the lack of balance, because the submission was being applied from the bottom up rather than the top down.

In other words, emphasis was placed on the submission of followers and almost none upon accountability of

7

leaders. In effect, the need to conform was passed down the 'pecking order' until the burden of compliance was heaviest at the bottom where responsibility is least.

While Church leaders were on the right track, there was a lack of wisdom in implementing a concept that had so much potential for problems. And so, just as with any truth carried to extreme, submission teaching became distorted and went into error. The cure was ultimately as deadly as the disease. The effect was a distortion of the whole biblical concept of submission. As a result, the legacy left to us is a concept of submission that sees it as a pain to be avoided rather than a healing truth to be embraced—as an exercise in love and freedom.

Submission as Freedom and Truth

Freedom is desirable but without self discipline and responsibility, it easily turns into self-serving rebellion. The individual becomes sovereign and chaos reigns. But submission, without knowing your privilege to choose or reject according to God's laws of relationship, becomes surrender of individuality. It leaves its followers in bondage to the limitations of the human understanding of leaders, which often results in mental, emotional, and spiritual bankruptcy. When the blind follow the blind, both fall into the ditch.

On the surface, freedom and submission appear to be opposites— desirable and undesirable. But in the hands of the One who created us and gave guidelines for living, they become perfect compliments to each other.

Jesus promised freedom through knowledge of the truth. He said, ""If you hold to my teaching, you are really my disciples. Then you will know the truth, and the truth will set you free" (John 8:31-32). Truth is not simply accurate facts but is true living as embodied perfectly in Jesus. He said, "I am the way and the truth and the life" (John 14:6).

Our Lord exemplified the perfect union of freedom and submission. He said, "For I have come down from heaven not to do my will but to do the will of him who sent me" (John 6:38). Through obedience to His Father's will, He demonstrated perfect submission, and perfect freedom when He *willingly* came and *willingly* submitted.

Power, Love, and a Sound Mind

If we are to learn submission from Jesus, there are laws relating to His love that we need to know. One is that "There is no fear in love. But perfect love drives out fear" (1 John 4:18). Another is that "God did not give us a spirit of timidity, but a spirit of power, of love and of self-discipline" (2 Timothy 1:7). God gave us His power first, so we can safely give ourselves to love without fear. Conversely, fear cannot operate in an atmosphere of love. Where there is love, there is no fear.

When responsibility and accountability are in place, love can flow, trust is possible, and fear is removed. We need not only to be able to love but also to feel loved. That assurance of being loved will cast out fear and we will feel empowered to take risks in reaching out to others. When fear is gone there is also freedom to embrace the Holy Spirit and the Word as your final authority.

The Place of Authority

God instituted authority in four areas:

Scriptures * Family * Church * Civil

9

Each will be discussed in succeeding chapters. Suffice it to say here that each has a place in our responsibility to live godly lives. Each one of us needs to operate in responsibility and with accountability. At all rungs on the submission ladder, danger signals should go up when accountability is lacking or removed.

If the authority over you is ungodly, you may find yourself in a hard place and suffering as you take a righteous stand. If so, know that spiritual depth grows out of times of trouble as roots grow in darkness. Christian character is developed in the valleys, not on the mountain tops. Since the first day of the Church, times of persecution and hardship have been the proving ground upon which she has walked in victory and grown in strength. But make sure when you suffer that you're suffering for righteousness sake and not for your own wrong doing (1 Peter 2:20).

Although the Word teaches that we are to respect those in authority, when there is a conflict in commands between the Word of God and the word of man, we are to obey God rather than man. He honors respectful disobedience for the right reason. God's will takes precedence over everything else. The Lord said to pray, "your will be done on earth as it is in heaven" (Matthew 6:10).

The structure of the earthly order of submission and authority is designed to emulate the heavenly order where God's word is absolute. Because of sin, however, man's effort toward absolute rule over the earth—or even over himself—is doomed to collapse. So God's redeeming power must intervene. His plan is that He is to be the only absolute authority over His Kingdom on earth, just as He is over His kingdom in heaven. We don't see it yet because He has limited Himself to accessing earth through His Kingdom in our hearts, and our hearts are not yet given totally over to Him.

Requirements of Authority

To understand authority from God's point of view, let's look at the story of the Centurion who came to Jesus for healing of his servant. The story will help us understand the meaning of authority from the position of the one exercising it.

> When Jesus had entered Capernaum, a centurion came to him, asking for help. "Lord," he said, "my servant lies at home paralyzed and in terrible suffering."
>
> Jesus said to him, "I will go and heal him."
>
> The centurion replied, "Lord, I do not deserve to have you come under my roof. But just say the word, and my servant will be healed.
>
> For I myself am a man under authority, with soldiers under me. I tell this one, 'Go,' and he goes; and that one, 'Come,' and he comes. I say to my servant, 'Do this,' and he does it."
>
> When Jesus heard this, he was astonished and said to those following him, "I tell you the truth, I have not found anyone in Israel with such great faith.
>
> (Matthew 8:5-10)

The Centurion said, "I myself am a man under authority," indicating that he understood who Jesus was and His relationship to God. By his statement he acknowledged his awareness of the responsibility that is essential to proper handling of authority.

Proper authority begins with the one who is to exercise the authority fully submitting to all that the responsibility of authority requires—including being accountable to a higher authority. Everyone needs to be accountable to someone, and all are ultimately accountable to God. To accept the conditions that go with a position of authority is to accept the accountability and responsibility that also go with the position.

It's no small thing to assume the responsibility of leadership. Success requires preparation, resources and commitment. For instance, as choir director in a small church I was given full authority over the choir by the pastor. I accepted the responsibility of that authority and committed myself to do my best. Once I made the commitment, I had to follow through with the details necessary for the choir members to trust my leadership. All the while, I was accountable to the pastor, who was ultimately responsible for the choir as part of the church ministry. He, in turn, was accountable to God for the spiritual needs of the congregation.

The reason I consciously and deliberately committed myself to the responsibility of the authority I had been given by the pastor was that I understood the meaning of "responsibility of authority," and something of the principle that guided the Centurion when he said, "I myself am a man under authority." Serving with responsibility constitutes the greater submission, even when you're in a position of authority and others are submitted to you.

Identifying Submission in Relationships

There are four parts or aspects to submission:

Submission to authority—love's response.
Responsibility of authority—love's commitment.
Accountability to each other—love's concern.
Accountability to God—love's source.

The cord that binds everything together in the submission/authority relationship is love. Love interlocks each level of submission and connects the whole to form a perfect unit. As we form and work thorough the relationships of life, we'll each find that we're sometimes in all three positions at the same time.

For instance, everyone has someone in authority to whom they submit. Everyone is in authority over someone—even if it's only yourself. And we all have God—to whom all must ultimately give account—in authority over us. It is He who guides us to assuming the responsibility for the choices we freely make. In that is submission with freedom. Just as Jesus came as a willing servant, godly submission makes of us willing servants, also.

The Mantle of Servanthood:
Submissive Living

God mandates that spiritual authority be exercised in the spirit of a servant. "The greatest among you will be your servant" (Matthew 23:11). A minister is by definition one who serves or ministers to others. The prophet Isaiah describes God's servant as one who is anointed of the Holy Spirit to bring truth and justice to all people (Isaiah 44:1). A God-anointed servant doesn't bring His message with a boisterous cry or the force of His personality. He ministers with compassion to those who are weak and struggling, in the same manner that the Lord did:

> A bruised reed He will not break, and a dimly burning wick He will not quench; He will bring forth justice in truth. (Isaiah 42:3)

God's servant offers healing and hope from the Creator of the universe to the bruised reeds and dimly burning wicks of this world—those whom life has crushed and whose light has been nearly snuffed out. Isaiah's prophecy applies to Jesus, the Messiah, and is also a charge to all who would serve in His name.

The mantle of authority with which God equips leaders that He has called will be in evidence when they minister. They will minister in the anointed spirit of a servant and with compassion toward hurting people for whom Christ died.

Who needs to submit to someone? We all do. We also need leadership that is accountable to others and to God, and the freedom to serve where God puts us.

****2****

Freedom in Submission to God

Defining Submission To God

There's a way to obey the authority over you without losing your sense of freedom. Make sure that submission is your idea by taking the initiative, do it for the right reason and purpose, and do it in love. If your submission is motivated by love, it will be in God's will and blessed by Him because God is love. And since the Holy Spirit will be working with you in that kind of submission, it will include freedom, for "where the Spirit of the Lord is, there is freedom" (2 Corinthians 3:17).

With that in mind, let's explore the meaning of submission. The dictionary defines submission as yielding to the power, control or authority of another; acquiescence or surrender. A working meaning for our purposes, and the one I like best, is *accepting the other person's definition of your relationship.* Keep in mind, however, that if your sense of what is right for you doesn't agree with the other person's expectation of you, then it would be unwise for you to submit to them. You only submit to those relationships that ring true and to which you agree.

As an example, let's look at God's definition of our relationship to Him, which is, "all have sinned and fall short of the glory of God" (Romans 3:23). From this we can see that initial submission to God requires you to agree with Him that you're a sinner— there's no question but that it's true, of course. If anyone knows, God knows.

As a sinner you're separated from God and cannot have a relationship with Him until you're reconciled to Him, and you can only be reconciled to Him by a savior—that is, by Christ.

> For if, when we were God's enemies, we were reconciled to him through the death of his Son, how much more, having been reconciled, shall we be saved through his life!   (Romans 5:10)
>
> All this is from God, who reconciled us to himself through Christ and gave us the ministry of reconciliation.   (2 Corinthians 5:18)

If you are to have God's life, you need the salvation provided by Christ. When you accept God's definition of your state as a sinner, confess your need of a savior and desire to change your relationship to Him, then Romans 10:9-10 becomes a reality in your life:

> That if you confess with your mouth, "Jesus is Lord," and believe in your heart that God raised him from the dead, you will be saved.

16

> For it is with your heart that you believe and are
> justified, and it is with your mouth that you confess
> and are saved.

When you've done what the above Scriptures say to do, God becomes your heavenly Father through the new birth, and Christ Jesus becomes your Savior and Lord. Obedience in your daily walk confirms His Lordship over your life.

To help you to willingly obey in all things, the Holy Spirit works in you to change your will so that you desire to do those things that are pleasing to God (Philippians 2:13). As your will continues to surrender to the will of God, submission to Him becomes a pleasant and joyful way of life. Additionally, the Holy Spirit guides your pathway and opens God's word to your understanding.

Applying The Definition To People

Whatever God says about our relationship to Him is true, but this is not always so with people, and you must judge carefully the right or wrong of every relationship before you submit to anyone. Your relationship to God, through the Holy Spirit, will help you to decide whether to accept a relationship with people. Remember, to "accept" is to make a choice—and if you're free to accept, you're also free to reject. It's your responsibility as a Christian to decide what you're willing to live with and what is godly and wise. Let the love of God and the principles of His kingdom be your standard and you won't go wrong.

If something is required of you that violates your conscience or is against God's will as written in His Word, then withdraw. Submission to God is the higher

17

law that rules above everything, and nothing can be allowed to interfere with that. Before you reject submission, however, seek godly counsel and pray so that you'll make a righteous judgment.

Whatever you do, don't base your judgment on whether the submission is convenient or comfortable to you or whether it's going to cost you something. Jesus' submission to His Father was costly, but He endured the cost by looking to the joy that was set before Him—and, as it will always be with us, His rewards were greater than the cost.

Jesus is Our Example

When Jesus died on the cross for the sin of the world, He demonstrated the ultimate in submission to the requirement of His Father's love. From the foundation of the world, God decreed that the price to be paid for sin was a blood sacrifice (Leviticus 17:11). Sin cannot co-exist with God's holiness, yet His love could not let mankind go without redemption (John 3:16).

But sinners cannot pay for their own sins—their sins make them unworthy to do so. Only One who never sinned could sacrifice His life for others. In the Old Covenant, the lambs without spot or blemish that were sacrificed under the Law pre-shadowed the Messiah to come. In the New Covenant, the unblemished Lamb of God shed His blood on Calvary's Cross and finished the work of reconciliation that the blood of all the sacrificed animals could never finish (Hebrews 9:12).

When the Son of God agreed to leave heaven and become flesh and be that sinless sacrifice, He demonstrated the ultimate in submission to His Father and to the need of humanity. He submitted out of

18

obedience to the Father's plan because of His great love, and the great need of all people for the salvation that only He could provide. There was no other way for us to be saved from sin and its penalty of eternal death. The Son's submission to His Father is an act of love for His Father and for lost humanity.

In Christ's unconditional love toward you, He has proven that your submission to His Lordship is safe. To accept and acknowledge His work on the Cross as payment for *your* sin makes Him your Lord. To continue on that pathway, however, requires walking "in the light, as He is in the light" (1 John 1:7). When you do that, you enter into fellowship with others who also have accepted a relationship with Him. The Christian Church is a blood-bought family of believers.

Does that Church relationship include *unquestioning* obedience to those in organizational authority over you? In the light of the Apostle Paul's teaching, some think so. He said, "Obey your leaders and submit to their authority. They keep watch over you as men who must give an account. Obey them so that their work will be a joy, not a burden, for that would be of no advantage to you" (Hebrews 13:17). There's a difference, however, between submission and obedience. Submission is an attitude while obedience is conduct. To be wise in our conduct, we need to understand the place of both.

Submission almost always includes obedience. But there is a delicate balance between responsibility for righteousness in your submission, and obeying those who have rule over you. The only way you can properly maintain that balance, is by submitting to God and letting

Him guide you by His Word and through the Holy Spirit. He will give you wisdom (James 1:5) and set you free to respond in love to what the need is. One of God's main concerns is for harmony among His family of believers

Look in your Bible at the context of Paul's words. As you can see, Paul was writing to the fledgling Jewish Christian church about dangers to which they were vulnerable. He was writing to people who were being severely tempted to leave Christianity and go back into Judaism.

The Christian way had encountered persecution and the wavering of many converts. There was also the confusion that accompanied the changes they had seen in God's way of relating to them— first the traditions of their forefathers and the Mosaic Law, and now Christ and the way of the Cross—to see it all as God's plan. Adding to the confusion were those from Judaism who were infiltrating the Church to prey on the weakness of new Jewish converts and pull them back under the Old Covenant Law. Also to convince Gentile converts that unless they came under some part of the Law they could not truly be saved.

These Judaizing teachers (Galatians 4:17) were bent on destroying the freedom the new Christians had in Christ. Their goal was to undermine and destroy this movement that had dealt a severe blow to the Jewish tradition through Christ's followers.

Paul's concern was that the Judaizers would influence his new Christians to go back to Abrahamic circumcision and the Mosaic Law. He reminded them that, since Jesus covered it all on the cross, that was no longer God's way. He pointed out that their freedom was based on Christ, who fulfilled for them the demands of the Law with its righteousness by works, and warned them that if they went back under the bondage of the law Christ would profit them nothing (Galatians 5:1-2). They were to live by life in the Holy Spirit, in contrast to the dead works of the Law.

In the first two chapters of his epistle to the Galatians, Paul explained to them that the New Covenant leadership of the Church, and especially his apostleship, was ordained by God. It was given for the teaching of sound doctrine to set their feet on solid ground, securing them on the new and better way.

The New Testament Scriptures had not yet been written, so these new Christians were dependent on the spoken word of their leaders for the teaching of sound doctrine. To follow the Judaizers would have destroyed the work of Christ for them. Therefore, if they were to continue in Christ, it was important that they give heed to their God-given leaders for protection from being led astray.

It was essential that the early Christians find leaders they could trust, and it's essential that we do the same today. Those who have successfully walked the way before us know the signposts we need to follow. It's wise to listen to them. Through these people Jesus has given gifts to the Church, which is the structure through which He performs His work. He is the Head, the Church is His body. Everything channels down from the Head through the various parts of the Body—and then out to the world as it suits His purposes. Within His Church, the Lord gives spiritual authority and directs His ministers through the anointing of the Holy Spirit.

Release and Empower

To maintain the anointing of the Holy Spirit, a God-given ministry must continually be submitted to God. As this is done, God will keep the minister's vision fresh with new insights for *people possibilities*, which will include those people He is raising up for leadership roles.

A forest can only survive if new trees continually develop and grow, and the Church can only survive if new leaders continually develop and grow. But problems often develop within a local church because those whom God is raising up as leaders sometimes attract a following because of a vision God has given them, and the drive He has given them to pursue it. Rather than recognizing the ministries forming within their congregations as being of God, however, many church leaders see them as disruptive and threatening and do all they can to subdue them or even drive them out of the church.

What they should do, of course, is make room for them, and not lose their God-given contribution to the Church. Those new leaders being raised by Christ in His Body need to be trained, released into ministry and then empowered to take leadership, whether at home or in forming another local church. A tree grows and spreads and brings many under its shade not by crowding all of its growth into its trunk, but by developing many branches that spread out their leaves as far as possible. So it is with a local church. It grows best— and serves best the work of Christ—by developing other local churches and spreading itself as far as possible.

Many potential pastors and lay leaders have been unnecessarily lost to the Church because of the reluctance of established local church leaders to share the spotlight, and their seeing the developing leaders as competition rather than new ministers of

Christ. If the established leaders feel there is danger of these new leaders leading people astray with wrong doctrine, then it should be dealt with by confrontation and teaching (Acts 18:24-26), not by destroying new ministries that Christ is raising. Losing such ministries has weakened many churches and limited the spread of the Gospel.

Committing Others to God's Care

The revolving door syndrome in churches needs to be carefully examined and dealt with in a Christ-like way. Contrary to the opinion of many Pastors, committed Christians don't leave a church without paying a heavy personal and spiritual price.

Even so, it's unusual for them to be contacted by a concerned Pastor who is interested in knowing why they left. It's almost as if the Pastor is afraid to know why for fear it has something to do with him, he doesn't care enough about them or their reason for leaving, or he is antagonistic to their leaving and so has rejected any further association with them. Perhaps he feels rejected.

Whatever the reason, many who left local churches could have contributed to the health of the Body of Christ if someone had been interested enough, and Christ-like enough, to listen to them. And even if the situation that caused them to leave can't be removed, surely it can be resolved without breaking fellowship. If you can restore them, restore them in gentleness (Galatians 6:1)—if you can't restore them, release them in love that they can feel.

To release a person in love is to trust God's care of that person's life. Quite often it boils down to this question,

"Do I really believe that God will be God in that person? Can I trust Him to take over where I must leave off and work out what is needed from here on?"

The more you love someone, and the more you have invested of yourself in that person's life, the more you're tempted to continue to exercise authority in a way that becomes control. Authority and control are not the same, just as submission and subjection are not the same. Knowing the difference and living accordingly sets the tone for a right balance between authority and submission

Watch as people begin to grow toward spiritual maturity. If they're not given freedom to make mistakes and return in acceptance and restoration, they'll have difficulty proceeding on to wholeness. In being given a challenge to grow, and being free under Christ to choose their path, people find significance and meaning that holds them steady.

God created us with a free will. He allows us to make wrong choices so that our right choices will have meaning. That means, of course, if we are free to be good, we are also free to be bad. So for those who make wrong choices, God makes a way of restoration. If God does that, shouldn't we also do it among ourselves? Shouldn't the ways of God be our ways? If so, we should never let people go without knowing there's a place of love and restoration awaiting them in our fellowship.

Building Trust

Submission to God should be first in all our dealings with people. He guides us into relationships that honor Him and provides freedom for everyone so exercised. Although many don't realize it, often both the person in authority and the person in submission attempt to control each other, and neither allow the other one to be totally free under God. But you cannot exercise godly authority unless you release to God the person over whom you have authority, and you cannot exercise godly submission unless you release to God the person to whom you are submitting. Both authority and submission are acts of love empowered by trust—first love and trust toward God, and then love and trust toward the other person, trusting God in them.

There is freedom and victory in releasing each other. Conversely, there is frustration and defeat in refusing to release people and relationships that you cannot improve by holding on.

Authority Figures

Often, especially when we're new Christians, our relationship to God as authority is molded by our relationship to the primary authority figure in our childhood. We'll often see our heavenly Father as we've seen that person—usually as we've seen our earthly father. So if obedience to parents as a child grew into willing submission as an adult, it will be easier for us to submit to God because of learned trust and obedience to authority.

I was blessed to be raised where trust came easily. My mother was a good example of selfless love and devotion as she trained her children. She was a wise and godly woman who gave me a solid foundation on which to build my life. She taught me by her example how to submit to righteousness in the midst of problems and wait for the rewards. Then after her training was finished she released me to discover for myself how freedom and responsibility work together.

Later, when my own mother was three thousand miles away and I had become a Christian, my mother-in-law was my spiritual mother as well. She taught me, by the way she lived and from the Word, how to live a Christian life in a practical and joyful way in spite of the legalistic tendencies of our church. She taught me to recognize the wholeness and freedom that a close relationship to God gives. I was trained in her kitchen and I shall always be thankful to God for her influence in my life. She, too, knew how to release others.

When we feel the freedom that God gives us as we release one another, we feel an increased ability to obey His command to love one another. When He gave that command, He knew what was necessary to make it possible. Jesus said, "Take my yoke upon you and learn from me, for I am gentle and humble in heart, and you will find rest for your souls. For my yoke is easy and my burden is light" (Matthew 11:29-30).

When the yoke requires that we live out His love to a lost and dying world we need Him on the other side. Much of the world is not lovely, yet He still loves, and so must we. In the above Scriptures, He was saying that we can love the unlovely through His love, and that He can take care of any concerns that are submitted to Him.

Submission becomes a beautiful concept, and well worth pursuing as we see God's plan at work. His design for life gives freedom within the confines of responsibility and vigilance. He knows our weaknesses and will guide us past the pitfalls if we have faith and trust in His guidance.

****3****

Submission in the Church

Understanding Submission

God's plan for running the Church is unique among organizations of the world. The true Church is a living organism, held together by the Holy Spirit's work in a blood-bought family. As for its operation, the Church is neither a democracy nor an autocracy—it's a theocracy. It's under the authority and guidance of Jesus Christ who delegates authority through the Holy Spirit to chosen servants for the purpose of making disciples. It was so in the beginning of the Church; it is so now.

Authority and submission are essential to the Spirit's ability to guide and lead. However, with the wrong use of the areas of dominion that Christ delegates in the Church, the exercise of authority can easily become domination and control. We were created neither to dominate others nor to be dominated by them but rather to submit to each other in the love of God. Since submission is a command to the Church, we need to understand why it was given as well as how to use it wisely.

Recognizing Problems

Problems can be found in the best of Churches. Many people are following the pastor to find more of Christ rather than following Christ and looking to a pastor for guidance. The first is religion, the second is relationship.

Our Lord is interested in relationship, not religion. If He had been willing to settle for religion He would have left the Pharisees alone. They were expert religionists. They demonstrated that a spirit of religion is a favorite tool of the enemy.

The devil keeps God's kingdom continually under siege. But God provides protection by calling and anointing ministers to guide His people away from Satan's snares. They're responsible for caring about the spiritual welfare of the members of the Church (Hebrews 13:17).

While some ministers are wise stewards of that call, some are not. You must discern the difference so you don't support the wrong ministers. How do you decide? There are some things you should keep in mind.

Leaders need followers—but leaders also need to be followers of, and accountable to, a higher authority. Followers need leaders who know where they're going, and who are certain that the destination is of God. The best example of a good leader who is God-anointed and directed is Jesus of Nazareth.

Jesus, the Good Shepherd

In John 10:14, Jesus said, "I am the good shepherd; I know my sheep and my sheep know me." As a sheep follows his shepherd, so must we follow Jesus and those through whom He leads. That's the submission He requires of us. His relationship with His own is personal—He doesn't have a substitute, someone who replaces Him. He also says that a hireling—someone who works for selfish reasons—will flee when danger comes, but a good shepherd will lay down his life for the sheep. Jesus thus declares a principle of servant leadership.

Psalm 23 and Ezekiel 34 are examples of seeing God's people as sheep. In the natural, the shepherd's job is to lead his sheep to food and water, protect them from pestilence and danger, and care for the sick and injured. The flock doesn't move until the shepherd does, he goes before them and they follow. When they stop to graze, his attention is solely on them and for them. He doesn't force them to eat, but leaves them free to feed unrestricted in the pasture he has chosen.

If a sheep wanders away into dangerous territory, the good shepherd pulls it back to safety with the crook of his staff. If one persists in straying to its own hurt, the shepherd sometimes has to break its leg, then carry the sheep in his arms while it heals. It is then forever faithful to stay near him (reminiscent of the Genesis account of Jacob's crippled hip—Genesis 32:24-32).

Spiritually, the breaking of the leg and use of the staff that brings one back, must be left to the True Shepherd. The Holy Spirit then guides the under-shepherd to carry out the hands-on work necessary for restoration. Since it is the nature of sheep (and people) to follow their leader, most of the flock require no such drastic action.

Think of your pastor. Can you see the way of a true, God-appointed, shepherd in him? Does he reach out with a healing touch to people who have problems, either in or out of the church? Can you support him as he cares for others without idolizing him? Consider those things as you pray for him.

If you're a pastor, do you follow the way of a shepherd? Can all your people safely trust your leadership? Do you trust your people? If not, why not? Can you release them into leadership of their own without feeling threatened? Mutual trust makes mutual submission possible.

Leaders who play to their followers feed weakness.

Leaders who play to potential leaders feed new leadership and growth.

Which do you do?

The Call of the Pastor

A pastor is called to a shepherding ministry in a local church. While his function is that of a hands-on caretaker of the flock, it's important to keep in mind that He does so only under the guidance and leadership of the Good Shepherd, Christ Jesus. A pastor's shepherding position is that of an under-shepherd. He's called to willingly and unselfishly care for and protect the flock that belongs to the Chief Shepherd. In his calling, he's not to look for material or social rewards here on this earth, but those eternal rewards that Christ will give him in the ages to come.

> Keep watch over yourselves and all the flock of which the Holy Spirit has made you overseers. Be shepherds of the church of God, which he bought with his own blood.

I know that after I leave, savage wolves will come in among you and will not spare the flock.

(Acts 20:28-29)

Be shepherds of God's flock that is under your care, serving as overseers—not because you must, but because you are willing, as God wants you to be; not greedy for money, but eager to serve;

not lording it over those entrusted to you, but being examples to the flock.

And when the Chief Shepherd appears, you will receive the crown of glory that will never fade away.

(1 Peter 5:2-4)

A pastor-shepherd is under submission to the same True Shepherd as the rest of the people. He is only one of five ministry gifts to the Church. Unfortunately, and unscripturally, today the other ministry gifts are not recognized in most churches, and where they are recognized they are almost always subjugated to the pastor.

The five gifts in combination are supposed to equip the saints to do the work of the ministry. In addition, there are the congregational gifts listed in Romans 12 and in 1 Corinthians 12. These, when recognized and put in place in a local church, provide the leadership and help from the congregation that the pastor needs to enable him to properly perform his shepherding duties. According to the Scriptures, all believers have gifts, so there should be a place for everyone in the local church to function in their gifts and know that they are contributing to the work of the Lord.

People need to be encouraged to teach and lead each other so that it is not all left to the pastor. When he welcomes their help without allowing it to threaten his power base, everyone benefits and the church will grow. Sheep beget sheep and nurture each other. The pastor's place is to give freedom for new life and encourage leadership among them. Not all pastors seem able to do this. Those who cannot, should carefully consider why it is that Christ trusted them enough to delegate authority to them, but they do not trust members of their own congregations enough to delegate authority to them.

It has been my observation in years past that people with the most potential for leadership are often squelched rather than trained to fulfill their potential. Such squelching is often a sign of a pastor with a problem. The result has been displaced, wounded soldiers, weakened and dying churches, and pastors who are eventually overworked and discouraged.

Often a pastor blames the congregation for it's failure, not fully aware of his part in it. He has been diligently doing what the system demands, never rising above it to touch the heart of the True Shepherd, bringing balance and full participation in the purpose of the church.

Understanding the Pastor's Role

When a pastor carries total authority and responsibility for the operation of the church, the power he holds is potentially dangerous. When it's submitted to the authority of the Holy Spirit, it will be kept on track by submission to others through accountability. Beware of inappropriate control. More about that later.

Accountability is the watchword. Strong, gifted leaders, willing to take the risk of releasing others to lead will not need cookie-cutter people, nor need to surround themselves with yes-men. A pastor who can lead without controlling people is a good man who deserves your support and prayers. You're in the Lord's battle together and he's on the front line, vulnerable to all sorts of attacks never seen by the congregation..

Don't criticize your pastor unless it's with tears and in prayer. Confront him if you need to, but be sure it's in loving concern with hope, not in condemnation and rejection. Be willing to learn from him. Surprise him by asking how you can help.

It takes unconditional love and trust in God to pour your life into people and then release them. To let go is not to care for but to care about. It's not to be protective but to let others face reality as they learn to stand on their own.

Teaching and exhorting one another to love and good works (Hebrews 10:24) are the only preventive measures by which we are to help others avoid pitfalls. God requires order to be imposed by the local church in matters of doctrine and morals after the fact; not by preset rules and laws to follow that inhibit personal responsibility and the resulting spiritual growth.

After they've been taught, responsibility demands that people be given freedom of choice with accountability. Teaching by word, however, is best confirmed by example. Children's lives are strongly influenced by the examples they see, and so are the lives of spiritual children.

Dangers of Wrong Submission

What do you do if you encounter a submission situation that is unscriptural and dangerous? To challenge wrong authority is sometimes seen as an act of rebellion while in fact, exactly the opposite is true. Spiritually, if a thing is not ultimately right for everyone, it is not truly right for anyone.

The Apostle Paul writes, "Brothers, if someone is caught in a sin, you who are spiritual should restore him gently. But watch yourself, or you also may be tempted" (Galatians 6:1). To allow sin to go unchallenged is to be false to your brother or sister.

Go with a humble spirit and in prayer—there is much at stake. And always remember, if we are to be sure of what is wrong we must first be sure of what is right. So "Do your best to present yourself to God as one approved, a workman who does not need to be ashamed and who correctly handles the word of truth" (2 Timothy 2:15). Be sure, however, that your 'sword of the Word' is wielded by the Holy Spirit (Ephesians 6:17).

There is a scriptural precedent for us in a situation Paul found at Antioch (Acts 15). Upon discovering the spiritual attitude of some who were in positions of leadership he "did not give in to them for a moment" (Galatians 2:5) so that the purity and truth of the Gospel would be preserved. He totally disregarded their position because he said, "God is not impressed with the positions that men hold *and* He is not partial *and* recognizes no external distinctions" (Galatians 2:6, AMP). When Paul found them to be false brothers, he quickly discerned what their purpose was—that of spying on their liberty in Christ Jesus so as to bring them again under bondage of the Law and under their control (Galatians 2:4).

Characteristic of human nature is the insidious desire of some to be in control, and of others to welcome that control. Without both of these weaknesses neither would be a problem. Those who allow or invite inordinate control to be held over them share responsibility with those who wrongly assume that control. Satan's greatest mischief is often on this very issue, because it interfers with the Lord's access to hearts.

Loyalty and love for a pastor is good, but it needs to be kept in perspective. Sometimes a church's adulation of the pastor, because of his charismatic personality, invites empire building. If that is a temptation, he can be his own worst enemy and the admiration of his followers a real danger for him. Even worse, the Lord's spiritual purpose for the church is then exchanged for a man's vision and purpose.

Control and Submission Gone Wild

The most flagrant example of this in recent times was that of Jim Jones and the blind loyalty of his followers, far beyond normal logic. Although he started with what appeared to be a good thing, it ended in the tragic deaths of nine hundred people in his Jonestown, Guyana, compound. He is, of course, the extreme example but it should serve as a warning against the evil inherent in human nature.

There is mischief waiting in the wings when people relinquish control of their lives to a man and lose sight of the Lord. No longer able to see truth, the resulting spiritual blindness characteristically leaves its victims unaware that they are blind.

Harriet's Story

When true believers experience this danger it will likely be in a church where the pastor's role is seen as akin to a monarch over a small kingdom. Submission to authority will be a key teaching and practice. This was the experience of a lady we'll call Harriet. It's a true story with the identifying details changed.

Harriet was a pianist and music director in a church just coming out of an older denomination gone sour. As the pastor responded to the Holy Spirit's call to change, he joined a fellowship of young churches, bringing a new freedom of worship. For a time they experienced growth, both in spiritual lives and in numbers. Then something changed. This is her story as she told it to me.

"As a girl I had experienced a lot of rejection and I took solace in developing my musical talent by playing the piano. When I was asked by my pastor at an early age to serve as pianist for our church I was elated. I took it as acceptance of me as I was, and my self-esteem soared.

"Later I was given the position of music director, helping guide the church through a precious time of revival. There were phenomenal demonstrations of the power of God in our midst. It was like walking in the continual presence of the Holy Spirit where love and submission came naturally. There were also Satanic attacks but God was always there to confirm His work.

"If the enemy can't get at us from outside, he will assume a disguise and attack from within. In this case the problem came in the form of an ambition to build a big church (the pride of life).

"For the Pastor it was a righteous desire to build God's kingdom. When the congregation went from one hundred to near one thousand, he envisioned two thousand.

"In the premature struggle for a building to house large numbers there was a lawsuit that exposed a major spiritual problem. The building had become more important than relationships with Christian brothers. In the disharmony that followed, the Holy Spirit was grieved and the glory cloud lifted but the ritual remained.

"The submission of one to another that had been so life-giving became only empty rules to obey or suffer the consequences. We began to worship the expression of worship rather than expressing worship to God. The music was planned the same and people continued seemingly unaware that something was amiss.

"It wasn't a complete loss for them, of course, because God honors worshiping hearts regardless of the surroundings. However, as the success of the services began to be dependent on our own efforts rather than the anointing of the Holy Spirit I felt strained both in spirit and in body.

"During the next two years, while the church continued to grow in numbers, the stress took its toll. I spent much time and money under the care of a doctor, all the while being taught that perhaps I was experiencing attacks from Satan because of our potential for success. I was, for my part, making unreasonable and unloving demands on those who served under me in the name of holding to a righteous standard.

"Eventually the tension began to break down the harmony of the staff and I began to question rules that would pit one against another while both were following what they believed to be orders from God. At that point I resigned and found myself struggling to get free of the lingering bondage.

"I was tormented by fear of a major tragedy in my life because I had left what I had been taught was the

37

'covering' of the ministry. Obedience to authority through the chain of command had been demanded, ostensibly to guard against the intrusion of evil. I was surely in disobedience to their authority.

"When the Lord began to set me free, I deliberately adopted a life style that would express my new-found freedom. I tested it by kicking off a few of the colloquial restraints I had been raised to believe were laws of God.

"It took three and one-half years of attending other churches and experiencing the healing of a loving Christian fellowship for my joy to return. Since learning to walk in freedom and truth, the joy of the Lord is now truly my strength and I have a much wider world in which to serve Him. I praise God for the healing of my spirit, scars and all. I know He will use my experiences to bring forth a better future."

The Solution and a Warning

Harriet's story points up the importance of living as true as we preach, of not allowing ourselves to be deceived by continuing the shell of God's plan without His power and presence. When the life of the Spirit is gone, the only thing left is dead ritual and rules, no matter how spiritual they may seem. When something dies it needs to be buried so resurrection life can come forth.

Conversely, the more God's presence is with us, the more carefully we must walk before Him. Our adversary, the devil, is always there "like a roaring lion looking for someone to devour" (1 Peter 5:8).

To avoid such problems, a pastor must be sensitive to the Holy Spirit and the needs of those in leadership. Worship and sacrifice go together and the pastor is the key. In this case, counsel with accountability could have headed off the problem and made way for the Holy Spirit to save a powerful ministry. It's God's work we're called to follow—we're not to go ahead of Him.

Submit to God and the Devil will Flee

What is submission to God? It's being obedient, even when it hurts. Submission to His will is to "offer your bodies as living sacrifices, holy and pleasing to God—this is your spiritual act of worship" (Romans 12:1). Being a sacrifice seldom makes you feel good. It requires getting out of your comfort zone and remaining eager to obey His Word without reservation. It's difficult, but the only alternative is disobedience.

When submission is adopted as a way of life, a continuing process of growth toward spiritual maturity follows. If you fail, try, try again. Remember, it's a process. The writer to the Hebrews says, "solid food is for the mature, who by constant use have trained themselves to distinguish good from evil" (Hebrews 5:14).

True submission and true humility go hand in hand. The Apostle James said, "God opposes the proud but gives grace to the humble. Submit yourselves, then, to God. Resist the devil, and he will flee from you. Come near to God and He will come near to you" (James 4:7-8). When you are under the covering of submission to God in Christ Jesus, the atoning blood of Calvary is your covering and that is the place of victory already won.

The Place of Submission

In conclusion, we need to recognize that God gives authority to church leaders so that He can work through them. They hold the gifts that are the channels between Christ and His Church (Ephesians 4:11-13). He provided a perfect system, even though it is subjected to imperfect humanity.

His plan is to have ministers who will speak His word, touch with His hands and feel with His heart. As this message becomes the focus of the Church, outreach ministry can come forth from its people. The world Jesus came to save will then witness a demonstration of His power and love.

When leadership is submitted to God and to serving the body of Christ, and when the church is submitted to God and to that leadership, there will be unity of spirit and purpose. With commitment to that purpose, the army of the Lord will be victorious.

Commitment is a rare commodity these days but that is what is needed—commitment to Christ and His body.

Submission is not easy, sacrifice is not easy, being a servant is not easy, but that's the way of a disciple of the Lord. It requires a willingness to get out of your comfort zone and move on with Christ.

Situations - Problems - Solutions

As you consider the following, think of the effect each solution would have on those involved. Which one would best be in alignment with "the Golden Rule" (Matthew 7:12)? You'll find that some are the reactions of a sinful nature.

Situation A: Joe is a former pastor in another state, seeking to fit into a congregation as a lay person and work under submission to the pastor.

Problem: Joe desires to serve God in support of the ministry, but his success with relationships and music appear to be a threat to the pastor. Because of some of the pastor's subtle sermon comments and his evasion of issues in the areas that Joe is involved, Joe feels the pastor is trying to maneuver him out of any ministry, maybe even out of the congregation. It appears to have happened to others.

Possible solutions for Joe:

1.) Try discussing the problem with the pastor, identify problems and work toward resolution. If that doesn't work . . .

2.) Resign position and sit quietly in meetings, pray for God's help, and wait.

3.) Find another church and start the process over again.

4.) Leave and pray for God's direction.

Without the cooperation of the Pastor, none of these is entirely satisfactory. Starting over is crippling.

Possible actions for pastor:

1.) Go to Joe to find out what troubles him, (if you don't already know). Try to understand the problem as he sees it, reconciling with him, in honesty and love. Consider giving him a place to work, thus preserving the relationship and strengthening your ministry.

2.) Be open to receive Joe when he comes to discuss the problem as he sees it.

3.) Resist communication with him to avoid stirring up trouble.

4.) Accept Joe's resignation without question and assume no part in it.

The responsible course to take is either 1 or 2. Both 3 and 4 may be easy ways out, but they are unhealthy for everyone.

Situation B: After dedicating her life to the Lord, Sue went to Bible School to train, then began attending a local church. She was told by the pastor that because she was a woman, there was no place for her to be in the leadership for which she was prepared.

Problem: Does Sue submit to his evaluation of the place of women or decide he is wrong and find another place where she is welcomed according to her abilities?

Possible solutions for Sue:

1.) Try persuading him to see her potential, as well as that of all women.

2.) Challenge the pastor's position and his authority to enforce what she sees as wrong. Without the Lord changing his mind this would cause trouble, doing damage to the cause of Christ. Not really an option.

3.) Since the pastor is adamant in his belief that he is right, and accepting his verdict is opposed to her convictions, leave without challenging it and try to find another church where her abilities will be used.

4.) There are many ministries who welcome the leadership of dedicated and trained women. Find one—or create one—and go to work.

Possible solutions for the pastor:

1.) Study the word as to the place of women in the life and ministry of Jesus. Study the ministry of women in the powerful Pentecostal outpouring at it's beginning. What God blessed then, He still blesses.

2.) Re-visit the scriptural position. Look at it from the position of current require-ments of women. Pray for a solution that does not include rejection.

3.) Keep a valuable worker and increase the church's ministry to the congregation.

4.) Judge her to be out of order to have prepared herself for this kind of service, and accept the loss of what may have been a dedicated worker.

Surely God's Word has a solution that will clear up this situation.

4

Submission Unifies the Church

Coming Together

In the book of Ephesians, Chapter 4, Paul emphasizes the importance of spiritual unity among believers. He said, "As a prisoner for the Lord, then, I urge you to live a life worthy of the calling you have received. Be completely humble and gentle; be patient, bearing with one another in love. Make every effort to keep the unity of the Spirit through the bond of peace" (Ephesians 4:1-3).

Without peace within the hearts of individuals the Church is weakened. Without peace between people, unity of spirit will escape you. Therefore, in the interest of bringing peace, ministering to the problems of individuals is a must. For most Churches that is a bit overwhelming because of the many problems people bring with them into their Christian life. For that reason some of the responsibility for personal disciplining, except for dangerous situations, should be extended to selected lay people. If it is limited to a pastor's time schedule, much of the need may go unmet. Often there are people who need to be released into this kind of ministry and empowered to do it. Showing that someone cares enough to listen and pray through emotional difficulties can be the thing most needed to help troubled Christians.

Personal peace is centered in the emotions, which is part of the soul, while unity is in spiritual bonding with others. Therefore, the whole person, spirit, soul, and body is involved in the Church 'growing up into' Christ, or coming into maturity. As I mentioned before, maturity is described to the Hebrew Christians as learning good from evil "by constant use" (Hebrews 5:14); in other words, by experience. You are then no longer susceptible to deception but can be guided by truth.

The Apostle Paul said, "speaking the truth in love, we will in all things grow up into Him who is the Head, that is, Christ. From Him the whole body, joined and held together by every supporting ligament, grows and builds itself up in love, as each part does its work" (Ephesians 4:15-16).

Speaking truth means being transparent with each other. Speaking in love makes it safe to be vulnerable and provides an atmosphere in which to develop maturity. If you know you're loved, you can risk being exposed for correction when it's necessary. You can also expect encouraging support when it's warranted. That's true body ministry.

Love at work

Love that brings unity to the Church is not essentially a good feeling, although good feelings will follow. Nor is it affection, although affection often demonstrates the feelings of love. It is, rather, the fruit of a loving relationship with Christ and an attitude we choose to hold toward others. Love is the character of Christ Jesus being formed in us.

Love does not begin with emotion but with a decision of the mind and a heart willingness to let the supernatural fruit of the Spirit rule. The battle will be won or lost in the mind and the heart.

Examine your life under the microscope of the message in the love chapter (1 Corinthians 13). There you will discover how dependent you are on the Spirit of God to obey the commands of the Lord to love one another. Supernatural love—love that is greater than our natural ability—which is the kind that is needed, comes when sought by faith and prayer, and is one element of the fruit of the Holy Spirit that Paul listed in Galatians 5:22.

In his first letter to the church at Corinth, the Apostle Paul wrote:

> Love is patient, love is kind. It does not envy, it does not boast, it is not proud.
>
> It is not rude, it is not self-seeking, it is not easily angered, it keeps no record of wrongs.
>
> Love does not delight in evil but rejoices with the truth.
>
> It always protects, always trusts, always hopes, always perseveres.
>
> Love never fails.   (1 Corinthians 13:4-8)

This describes the attitude you commit to when you decide to love God's way. Inevitably, testing will follow as you rub elbows with other Christians whom God is also testing. Things won't always go your way, no matter how good your intentions, but you can still be happy. When everything is in the Lord's hands, everything is all right. Seeing others through His eyes does wonders for your attitude.

The testing and proving within close relationships will likely produce friction. Friction needs lubricating oil. The remedy for friction between people is the oil of the Holy Spirit, manifested through loving submission

The "Bursa" of The Holy Spirit

The lubricating and cushioning tissue (sac, or saclike cavity) between joints of the human body is called the bursa. It must be healthy in order to move without pain. If there is a sick joint, the whole body knows it, as anyone who has had bursitis (an inflammation of the bursa) can verify. In the same way the body of Christ is hindered if there is a 'sickness' in the relationship (the joint) between any two 'bones' (people)—especially that 'red-hot inflammation' that sometimes occurs between people, even Christians.

Godly—loving—submission is the Holy Spirit's bursa for the body of Christ. The bursa lubricates and cushions the joints of the human body so the bones can work as extensions of each other. Loving submission lubricates and furnishes the cushion for the work of the Holy Spirit in the body of Christ. It's by learning to handle relationships with other people in the love of God that the body of Christ can function in unity.

To further illustrate, in a child's body, growth happens at the bone ends so they remain soft. Because of that, they are not yet sensitive to over-use and so they don't react in pain except under extreme conditions. Doctors warn that care should be taken not to overwork very young athletes, especially in track, because excessive running can damage the growing bones.

That warning also applies spiritually. Young Christians can be spiritually damaged if they're subjected to more demands in relationships than their maturity warrants. Concerning responsibility given too soon, Paul writes, "He must not be a recent convert, or he may become conceited and fall under the same judgment as the devil" (1 Timothy 3:6).

This lesson from friction and joints shows why Jesus put so much emphasis on forgiveness and love, also why leaders need wisdom. The process that provides the whole body with the necessary elements to grow up into Christ, the head of the Body (Ephesians 4:15), is a sensitive one.

As the Church comes to the place of unity and maturity for which the Lord Jesus prayed we will demonstrate to the whole world the pure bride without spot or wrinkle for which He is coming. Jesus prayed, "that all of them may be one, Father, just as you are in me and I am in you. May they also be in us so that the world may believe that you have sent me" (John 17:21).

The Koinonia (Fellowship) of Submission

The Greek word describing New Testament fellowship among the early Christian believers is *koinonia*. If we're to restore to our Christian relationships that which gave substance to theirs, we must learn from their example of honesty and humility. Jesus gave them a basic lesson in these two Christian virtues when He washed the disciples' feet:

49

When he had finished washing their feet, he put on his clothes and returned to his place. "Do you understand what I have done for you?" he asked them.

"You call me 'Teacher' and 'Lord,' and rightly so, for that is what I am.

Now that I, your Lord and Teacher, have washed your feet, you also should wash one another's feet.

I have set you an example that you should do as I have done for you.   (John 13:12-15)

John tells us that Jesus loved His own unto the end, or to the uttermost. The love and acceptance of Jesus knows no limits. Washing dirty feet was His way of teaching them through servant leadership about the ongoing need for spiritual cleansing throughout the daily walk of life, and helping each other to remain clean.

Dirty feet in need of washing should still evoke a call to us to present our lives for a spiritual cleansing of our walk. It means confessing our faults one to the other and living in transparency. Jesus commands it as an expression of the servant's heart among us. He's teaching the principle of personal accountability by a living parable.

As we recognize the faults and failures among us, our Lord calls us to a non-judgmental approach toward helping in the correction of them. Jesus did not condemn dirty feet, but He did insist on the washing, and then He said, "Do as I have done to you."

It was just after the Last Supper, His final time of fellowship with them before going to the Cross, that He began to wash the disciples' feet:

He came to Simon Peter, who said to him, "Lord, are you going to wash my feet?"

Jesus replied, "You do not realize now what I am doing, but later you will understand."

"No," said Peter, "you shall never wash my feet." Jesus answered, "Unless I wash you, you have no part with me." (John 13:6-8)

When we minister to others, if we encounter embarrassed pride as Jesus did in Peter, perhaps it's because the real need of the heart is being exposed. Ministering to needy hearts with the healing love of Jesus is the purpose of the exhortation and counseling ministry of the Church. His love in action is the means of developing a strong and lasting *koinonia* among believers. Yet not everyone is ready to pay the price for it. Some are still in process. God's love in us is patient.

The Cost of Discipleship

A church that neglects the opportunities to demonstrate the love of God is refusing to be salt and light to a world in decay and darkness. Godly submission will be a rare commodity in such a church. One is described in the vision given to John in Revelation 3:14-18. It was located at Laodicea:

To the angel of the church in Laodicea write: These are the words of the Amen, the faithful and true witness, the ruler of God's creation.

I know your deeds, that you are neither cold nor hot. I wish you were either one or the other!

51

> So, because you are lukewarm—neither hot nor cold—I am about to spit you out of my mouth.
>
> You say, "I am rich; I have acquired wealth and do not need a thing." But you do not realize that you are wretched, pitiful, poor, blind and naked.
>
> I counsel you to buy from me gold refined in the fire, so you can become rich; and white clothes to wear, so you can cover your shameful nakedness; and salve to put on your eyes, so you can see.

This church is not even aware of it's poverty, blindness, and nakedness. In fact, it's people are proud of their material abundance and seem to consider themselves to be without needs. Their smug satisfaction with material affluence blinds them to their spiritual poverty and their need for clear vision and clean robes. These are things that only Jesus as Lord of the Church can provide.

Is it possible that in our sufficiency we are the modern expression of that church? It's a sobering thought. If so, we need to know that He still extends His invitation to, "Buy from me gold refined in the fire." Gold is costly, the refining process burns away dross—Jesus offers it for sale if you're willing to buy.

How do you buy? You consider its worth and decide to give up something of value to get something you want more. What is keeping you from following closely with Jesus? In eternal coinage, it is worthless by comparison. The robes of righteousness to cover our sin nature and the healing salve that opens blind eyes are costly. They cost Jesus his life and He offers them to you freely. Your price comes in the willingness to identify with the Cross for your life. It's the bargain of the ages for you. True worship has from the beginning meant bringing a life-exchanging sacrifice. It still does. Neither God nor His ways have changed.

Ready For The King

As we approach the day of His coming, the unity of the Church is more essential than ever. Therefore, understanding the place of submission in relationships is more essential than ever.

When Jesus gave His disciples the parable of the ten virgins, He was giving a picture of the condition of the latter-day Church. He said:

> At that time the kingdom of heaven will be like ten virgins who took their lamps and went out to meet the bridegroom.
>
> Five of them were foolish and five were wise.
>
> The foolish ones took their lamps but did not take any oil with them.
>
> The wise, however, took oil in jars along with their lamps.
>
> The bridegroom was a long time in coming, and they all became drowsy and fell asleep.
>
> At midnight the cry rang out: "Here's the bridegroom! Come out to meet him!"
>
> Then all the virgins woke up and trimmed their lamps.
>
> The foolish ones said to the wise, "Give us some of your oil; our lamps are going out."
>
> "No," they replied, "there may not be enough for both us and you. Instead, go to those who sell oil and buy some for yourselves."

53

> But while they were on their way to buy the oil, the bridegroom arrived. The virgins who were ready went in with him to the wedding banquet. And the door was shut.
>
> Later the others also came. "Sir! Sir!" they said. "Open the door for us!"
>
> But he replied, "I tell you the truth, I don't know you."
>
> Therefore keep watch, because you do not know the day or the hour.   (Matthew 25:1-13)

These virgins represent the Church waiting for Christ to come for His bride (Ephesians 5:23). The parable says they all brought (burning) lamps but only half of them had sufficient oil for the long wait. While they all slumbered (half asleep) and slept (soundly), *all* of their lights went out.

At the call of the bridegroom they all trimmed their lamps, but for half of them it was a fruitless effort. There was no reserve oil, and no light. When they turned to other people who had brought oil it did no good because there was not enough to share. (The lamp is the human spirit (Proverbs 20:27), which is the vessel for the Holy Spirit.)

Apply this to the Church condition and the message is this: After a long wait (the first alert came with the outpouring of the Holy Spirit almost a century ago) the Church has, with few exceptions, fallen asleep.

In the parable, those who had a reserve of the Holy Spirit were taken, while those who did not were left. Does this indicate that it is dangerous to depend on someone else's experience with the Holy Spirit? While we need close fellowship with each other, each person must keep his own relationship with the Lord up to date. Joining with others to let their spirituality 'rub off' will not be enough. At the coming of the Lord, only an intimate relationship with Jesus Christ will count.

When they came to get Him in Gethsemane, Jesus said to the chief priests and others, "this is your hour—when darkness reigns" (Luke 22:53). To Pilate He said, "You would have no power over me if it were not given to you from above" (John 19:11). The Lord's apparent defeat was only to make way for the greatest redemptive victory known to man.

Paradoxically, that is also true of His Church. Since this hour of slumber is in God's timetable, the trimmed wicks will shine gloriously bright as the world gets darker. Then victory will swallow up defeat in the awakening that the Holy Spirit is preparing us for. Surely the Lord's return draws near.

Let's not get caught like the foolish virgins who were without their own oil. There will be no time to go out and buy when the bridegroom comes. Let's continually worship in the way that brings the presence of the Holy Spirit into our individual lives, rather than depend on others to make us spiritual. Church attendance and cooperate worship must not substitute for personal interaction with God.

A right relationship with God, however, always includes right relationships with other Christians, and the creation, thereby, of a true spiritual family. His plan is for a spirit of unity throughout the body of Christ. The closer we get to the coming of the Lord, the more we can expect Him to nudge us toward the unity for which Jesus prayed.

That will mean learning to live in submission one to the other because of His love to us, and then through us to each other. He calls us to purity so nothing will hinder our relationship to Him because He's coming for a glorious Church that is "without stain or wrinkle or any other blemish, but holy and blameless" (Ephesians 5:27b).

5

Authority vs. Control

Authority is in the Spirit

It was the authority with which Jesus spoke that caught the attention of those listening to His sermon on the mount. His manner of speaking was in sharp contrast to the rigid detail of the Law that the people were accustomed to hearing from the scribes. As recorded in Matthew's gospel, "the crowds were amazed at his teaching, because he taught as one who had authority, and not as their teachers of the law" (Matthew 7:28b-29).

A person who has an attitude of authority about him or her will soon have a following regardless of whether they're right or wrong. That attitude gives the impression that the person and the message are trustworthy and true, and so people are drawn to it.

That's the reason you must take responsibility for the decision to submit or not to submit to someone. Take time to check out the integrity of the message, as well as the trustworthiness of the person behind the message.

Scripture warns us of wolves in sheep's clothing that will come in and not spare the flock (Acts 20:29).

In this regard, Paul's instruction to Timothy applies to us as well : "Do your best to present yourself to God as one approved, a workman who does not need to be ashamed and who correctly handles the word of truth" (2 Timothy 2:15).

The New Testament Christians at Berea, "received the message with great eagerness and examined the Scriptures every day to see if what Paul said was true" (Acts 17:11). If we are careful to study the Scriptures and follow the Word as they did, we too will find the truth and be able to separate it from the things we hear and read that are not truth.

In his book, *People of The Lie,* Dr. M. Scott Peck, MD., discusses his work in dealing with people needing deliverance from evil power. He says, "I have learned these past years that evil—whether it be demonic or human—is surprisingly obedient to authority. Why this is so I do not know. But I know that it is so."[1] He also states that authority must be exercised in knowledge and love and requires enormous exertion.

Let us take note that for Jesus the anointing power of the Holy Spirit made bringing evil under control seem effortless. On the day of Pentecost, He transferred that power to His Church. Evil now bows to the authority of His name.

Perhaps the "why" that escaped Dr. Peck is that authority, which is a function of the spirit, was originally instituted by God who is a Spirit. He maintains control over that authority system as it continues to operate throughout the spirit realm. It's His provision for holding the kingdom of darkness at bay.

God's people have the privilege of being His emissaries of the system, the channels that He uses to perform His work on earth.

Evil will bow to the authority of the Holy Spirit's power as He operates through a human vessel to break the chains of bondage. Those chains are in the nature of evil, which always binds the person to itself. Good, on the other hand, lets the person be free to lovingly submit to the will of a loving Father.

The person who is free takes responsibility for himself rather than relinquish control to someone else. He is then free to be a channel for God's authority, neither controlling nor being controlled—because a controlling spirit is not from God.

God Gives Authority

Honoring authority furnishes structure to life. An authority system makes it possible for any society to proceed with order and grow in peace. Nothing is static. When growth stops there is death at work. Always there is change. It's so that He might participate in this change that God gives authority to man, then works through him.

His plan is to work through people, and He began it with the first man. When God placed Adam in the garden to tend it and gave him dominion over the earth, He also gave him responsibility to be head over Eve, his wife. This was God's first delegated authority. What He began, He has continued with consistency throughout the ages.

God established authority first in the home, then extended it to the Church and to government. In each of these places its success is determined by the way in which responsibility to others is handled. The position a person holds in an organization does not create authority in their spirit; it only gives it a channel through which to operate and fixes accountability.

How do you get a sense of being equipped with authority for your position? Good question. The authority of a parent, for instance, is God-given, but knowing how to use it is not. First learn to control your own spirit. Then find a purpose that is bigger than yourself, lose yourself in it, and learn all you can about it. As you conquer difficulties and gain self confidence, you'll find yourself speaking with authority in your chosen field.

Control

How can you recognize a spirit of control? A spirit of control is the result of trying to do or be something for which you feel—or are—inadequate. It's sometimes accompanied by a lust for power. Typically, you have to keep a tight rein on details, and are unable to share responsibility. Insecurity and fear of failure is at the root, often robbing you of the ability to trust others to do things right. This, in turn, robs you of their best effort.

When people are put in leadership without preparation for holding authority, they'll be at a disadvantage. Knowing something is amiss, they'll be tempted to function from a spirit of control. This is especially important for teachers. They need authority to keep control of a classroom, but if positive authority is not there, negative control is the substitute.

Authority of a Teacher

One of the finest teachers I have known was Chuck Oliver, ("Big 'O'" the kids called him). He was principal of a Christian High School where my son attended and I was a teacher. This man had such an attitude of authority that he had only to speak softly or give a penetrating look at his students to set them straight.

He was the heartbeat of the school. He commanded the respect of those teenagers, especially the boys. They loved him, respected him and learned from him. Now, years later, there are many of his former students who look back on their time under his leadership with gratitude. They appreciate him for being a man who taught love of God while he was teaching academics.

He was not fully aware of what made the difference between his success with the kids and that of other teachers. Although they were equally well qualified, some could not maintain the order necessary for good teaching. We discussed this and as I thought about it, I realized that here was a man whose sense of authority was well established in his spirit.

God knew when He called teachers that authority was necessary to successful godly teaching. He therefore made it a part of the gift package (Ephesians 4.11).

Control Harmful to Christian Schools

In contrast, I have seen others in the same position who operated in the spirit of control. They held a tight reign on behavior without reaching the hearts of students. The result was to destroy or weaken the schools with lasting negative results in the lives of the students.

Kids know they need rules and guidelines but they know, perhaps better than adults, what is fair and right. They need training that gives freedom for creative expression to try their wings among their peers. (They need to be given wings to soar above the crowd.)

In Christian schools I have been involved with, I have observed that those in charge who are causing the most damage seem to be the ones who make the best outward impression. Their main concern seems to be holding up a visible standard. They can't see beyond the immediate situation to judge long range results, which are often not good. As a result, some children graduate from the school vowing never to attend a church.

At best, Christian schools walk a fine line between authoritative discipline and legalistic control. Authority expressed in love builds character and lays a good spiritual foundation, while punitive discipline does not. When discipline through punishment is expected to turn out righteous kids, someone is in for a surprise.

There is still a need for effective discipline in schools, especially now. Small children feel safer when the adults in charge make rules that are fair, and see to it that they are obeyed. Young teens need firmness, accompanied by love and understanding of their particular needs, all with consistency.

Enforcing rules should apply to behavior that you can control. Trying to make people righteous by controlling their behavior is the wrong goal for Christian leaders. Rather, it should be to provide an atmosphere—through training in righteousness—in which the Holy Spirit is free to convict of sin and draw them to righteousness in Christ.

Where things of God are concerned, children need to be led instead of driven. Give the young a vision and a future. Let appropriate choices belong to them as an important part of growing up, allowing for consequences to drive home the wisdom of living by principles. In this way, they are being trained for responsible independence.

The Product of Christian Schools

These days Christian schools are, in most cases, a treasure. They have benefited from years of experience, and the ones who have succeeded are meeting a genuine need. As an alternative to increasingly problematic public schools, they can be a God-send. Godly people are working sacrificially to minister to children and they are to be commended. God bless them.

We need, however, to look also at the product of Christian schools from the perspective of those kids who fell through the cracks. The system is not without it faults, and not all its fruits are good. The authority/control issue is usually the culprit. When students see the system over them as teaching Christianity but without the love of Christ, they see rules without relationship, which, according to Josh McDowell, invites rebellion.

The leaders of the communist revolution in China, for instance, were the disillusioned product of missionary schools. To quote Winkie Pratney, "Most of the really dangerous radicals of our time are people who have given themselves to a religious cause that has been turned significantly to darkness."[2] He then says that most if not all confirmed atheists in the western world are people who have had some kind of church background.

Teachers and administrators have an awesome responsibility to be living examples of God's love and acceptance, without compromising with sin. Miracles happen when children know they're truly loved. They learn to relate to God's authority by the relationship they have with adults in authority over them. They need to see that Godly authority sets us free because it serves in love and offers forgiveness for wrong doing.

To Serve In Love

We are called to serve one another in love, to be submissive one to the other according to the need, and as unto the Lord. Needs take many forms and they are all around. There is a difference, however, between serving in love and serving because of the control (power) it gives you. The need of an infant or a handicapped person, for example, is for someone to do for him what he cannot do for himself. Whether submissive love or control is being expressed depends on the motive behind the help.

If the motive is control, then the one who has accepted being under control will, if he is an adult, be concerned about meeting the requirements of the person who is over him or her. The caretaker may feel too much burden, but feel that his or her usefulness is threatened if the control is relinquished, so independence is not encouraged.

In psychological terms this is called a co-dependent relationship—an unhealthy need for having someone dependent on you. Your way of feeling significant is to enable that person to continue being dependent, which perpetuates the problem. The Holy Spirit will you show a better way.

Everyone needs to do all they can toward independence. The Apostle Paul said it this way, "For God did not give us a spirit of timidity, but a spirit of power, of love and of self-discipline" (2 Timothy 1:7). In other words, the

Spirit that comes from God gives us the power to live in freedom and confidence—through which love can flow.

The Spirit of God doesn't condone rebellion against authority but He does enable you to go the extra mile when you encounter abuse of authority. Jesus told us how to handle control without sinning or surrendering when it is forced upon us: "And if someone wants to sue you and take your tunic, let him have your cloak as well. If someone forces you to go one mile, go with him two miles" (Matthew 5:40-41).

When Jesus said to go the extra mile and give him your cloak also, He was saying that when you submit to a demand it's in your power to do more than is asked. When it's a choice freely made in obedience to your heavenly Father, you've taken command of the situation and you're in control. That which you give willingly cannot be forced upon you. Your victory is found in joy because of love for God.

God's Timing

Whatever your mission, prepare yourself and trust God's timing, because if God begins a work in a person He is faithful to finish it. He will orchestrate the circumstances of your life to work out His purpose. Paul said, "being confident of this, that he who began a good work in you will carry it on to completion until the day of Christ Jesus" (Philippians 1:6).

Trust God and resist the temptation to run ahead of Him in your own effort to fulfill a vision. Otherwise, you may wind up on the back side of the desert like Moses and share in the lessons he had to learn.

65

Moses - Authority With Meekness

Moses was born in Egypt to godly parents who were Israelite slaves. Preserved from the slaughter of infant boys, raised in the palace as Pharaoh's son, and trained to be ruler of Egypt, the mantle of leadership was on him from birth. When he was a mature man of forty, he already knew that he was born to deliver his people from 400 years of Egyptian slavery

The problem was that he tried to do it without waiting for God's command. He killed an Egyptian who was mistreating an Israelite and had to flee for his life. He found himself on the back side of the desert among the Midianites, where he stayed forty years. It was from there, after having learned who he was *not*, that the Lord called him to go back to Egypt. In God's time, Moses was given all he needed to exercise God's authority in obedience.

Only then could he come into the fullness of who he *was*—only by following God could he lead His people out of Egypt. It was on this premise that the deliverance of the nation of Israel was to depend.

After his forty years in the desert, the eighty-year-old Moses led his people out of Egypt and slavery. He then exercised his authority in meekness as he took the nation of Israel through another forty years in the wilderness.

When the Israelites murmured and complained, Moses saw that it was not against him but against God who had called him. As such he did not take personal offense at them but took the problem to God and released it there. That is how meekness works. The Scripture says of Moses, "(Now Moses was a very humble man, more humble than anyone else on the face of the earth)" (Numbers 12:3). Meekness was his because he could see clearly how God keeps accounts for wrong doing.

After forty years of testing in the wilderness, the Israelites were ready to enter the Promised Land. Moses died at the age of one hundred and twenty years just before God told them to go over the Jordan river into Canaan. They went under a new leader: Joshua.

Occupying the Land

Exercising the authority of the believer is somewhat like the children of Israel entering the promised land under Joshua; God gave the land to them before they began to occupy it. They could not, however, enjoy it's blessings or make it theirs until by faith they went to battle and drove out the enemy. God did not do for them that which they needed to do for themselves.

They gave us the pattern we are to follow as we take the territory that He has promised to us in the spiritual realm. The territory we have been given is to be claimed as we step into the authority Jesus gave us through His name. We must fight in the prayer closet to win battles over the enemy internally before we can go into the world against the powers of darkness externally.

Every Christian has been given a degree of authority in the Holy Spirit. In His prayer for His disciples, Jesus prayed, " As you sent me into the world, I have sent them into the world" (John 17:18).

Jesus has sent us and we are to go. To follow God is to have the privilege of living in a realm of authority over the power of Satan in our lives, and over our own fallen nature. We still have the capacity to sin but we need not be enslaved by it. We have power over sin through the blood of Jesus, which is our cleansing and our victory. We are to overcome sin and our enemy "by the blood of the Lamb and by the word of [our] testimony;" and not love our "lives so much as to shrink from death" (Revelation 12:11).

Authority and control each have a place but it's good to see clearly which is to be used in a particular situation. Godly authority is characterized by His love, serving needs near to His heart. Earthly authority is characterized by upholding societal principles, often requiring control of a situation. Any situation is better served if it is understood in the light of God's order of authority.

[1]*People Of The Lie*, by M. Scott Peck, MD., (© Copyright 1983, Simon & Schuster, NY.).

[2] *The Thomas Factor* by Winkie Pratney. (© Copyright 1989, Chosen Books, Fleming H. Revel Company, Baker House Books, Grand Rapids, MI.).

6

Submission in Marriage

Marriage is a two-way street. We have heard much about women in submission to their husbands but little about the submission involved in the responsibility God puts on men. Actually, the higher command was given to a husband to love his wife as Christ loved the church.

Jesus' submission to serving the needs of the Church shows how a husband has his own kind of submission, that of submitting to the requirements of headship. As the God-designated head of the house, a husband is responsible to be provider, protector, and guide for his wife and family. Beginning with his name, he also gives the family its identity and sets the standards by which they live.

A wife helps to form those standards and put them to work. She then accepts responsibility for the atmosphere of the home her husband provides, and the care of family members. In this way, each marriage partner shares in submitting to the needs of the other. So you see, it's not only a wife's issue. Christ made it mutual, love makes it work.

Over-Emphasis of Wifely Submission

Wifely submission is valid and good, but the way that it's usually understood—and rejected—needs a fresh interpretation to line up with Biblical truth. God was not unaware of the issues we would face when He gave His instructions. There must be a key to making submission work for today's Christians.

Modern living often necessitates that women take a more visible role in contributing to the welfare of society and the family. As a result, the subject of submission has been brushed aside as unrealistic and unworkable. At those times when its one-sided interpretation has been taken seriously, it has led to unscriptural expectations and marital distress.

A common interpretation has been that the solution is for the wife to give unquestioning submission to her husband. She then can expect God to fix him as a reward for her obedience. The catch, however, is that God's command is to the husband is to take leadership, not to the wife to force him to it.

This pseudo-scriptural teaching would lead us to believe that it's always in the power of a wife to make her husband respond to God. The truth is that God does not violate anyone's free will. He only brings circumstances to bear in influencing change. It is the Holy Spirit's place to convict of sin and wrong patterns of living. God's command to a wife is to submit to her husband's needs (which translates into love), so God can work on him.

Actually, God doesn't always do what we prescribe for Him to do in the way that we expect. The soldiers in God's army must be volunteers. The only change a wife can compel is in herself, while releasing to God any changes in her husband. They should both be working to cultivate a submissive spirit through a relationship with Jesus.

Wives in Submission and Freedom

God's Word on submission given specifically for wives says: "Wives, in the same way be submissive to your husbands so that, if any of them do not believe the word, they may be won over without words by the behavior of their wives, when they see the purity and reverence of your lives. Your beauty should not come from outward adornment, such as braided hair and the wearing of gold jewelry and fine clothes. Instead, it should be that of your inner self, the unfading beauty of a gentle and quiet spirit, which is of great worth in God's sight" (1 Peter 3:1-4, NIV).

It may not appeal to a woman's pride to live in her husband's shadow, so to speak, but her place in his life is to complete him and strengthen him. To do that, her unique appeal is through the inner beauty God has given her and her ability to adjust to her husband's needs. God made men and women different in order to make the union complete. He then wrote the rule book on what is best for us. We can apply the rule of first occurrences in the Bible, showing us God's basic intentions for His plan for the sexes.

Husband Needs A Helper

God created man first—then woman to be a helper to meet his needs, a "help suitable for him" (Genesis 2:18). A man who is a strong leader is always made stronger by the support of a strong personality in his wife. If his need, however, is for her to take charge then that is right, and to do anything else would be subtle rebellion.

For instance, he may need her to take charge of handling finances. For her to insist that finances are his job because he is the head is not appropriate submission. His work may take him away for a time, in which case she needs to take charge of everything in the family. Any place he cannot or will not take leadership is a place for her to do her best to fill in.

If there is a need to establish basic principles of righteousness, however, her place is to hold the standard for herself. Then, within that framework, persuade him to change. If gross sin, such as physical abuse or criminal activity is involved, separation may be necessary. When you're not sure, submission to God's righteousness must be your guide.

Submission to righteousness could require that she refuse to be a part of that which is ultimately harmful to him as well as to her. Refusal may be necessary for her emotional and spiritual survival as well. "God has called us to live in peace" (1 Corinthians 7:15b). As a result, the marriage commitment may be challenged. In that case, going to a Christian counselor may help. But remember, in the end we will stand before God as individuals, not as couples.

Each of us will answer for our obedience to God with regard to relationships, including the marriage one. It's a sacred challenge and not always easy. Jesus made provision in Matthew 5:32 for the exceptional situation when He recognized a life given over to adultery as cause for putting away marriage vows.

God is always practical. When He gives a command, He gives the power to be obedient to that command and the result will be righteousness. Submission to righteousness sometimes requires speaking the truth in love and may necessitate confronting the problem head-on, but love necessitates that it be done in the spirit of meekness and humility. If the headship of man presents a problem, remember God has a reason for recognizing the man as head. He began life that way.

Life Began With Adam

God gave the seed of life only once. The spirit of man began with Adam and has been in continuous process ever since—through woman but not from her. The seed that produces children to perpetuate the human race is resident in the man only. According to geneticists, the male semen, which initiates life, contains the blood developing property for the new body that is being formed. Leviticus 17:14 tells us that, "the life of every creature is its blood."

The continuity of life seed in the man explains the reason why God places prime responsibility on man for the welfare and guidance of the family—he is key to the perpetuation of the human race. That He holds man in primary responsibility is clear all through the Old Testament in God's dealing with the family. He said of Abraham, "For I have chosen him, so that he will direct his children and his household after him to keep the way of the LORD by doing what is right and just, so that the LORD will bring about for Abraham what he has promised him" (Genesis 18:19).

Throughout Old Testament history, the principle of the head of the family being responsible for the whole was very clear as God formed His chosen people into a nation. Those ancient people have much to teach us in this regard.

One lesson we can learn from them is the fallacy of tradition. It was Jewish tradition, not God's law, that put

73

women in subjugation to men. They took the principle of male leadership to mean subjection of women and made it their law. Jesus changed all that by showing honor to women and the place they held in His earthly ministry. The Holy Spirit continues to validate that position. Let's not, however, throw out the baby with the bath water—the vital role of the headship of men in our time is emphasized in the final words of the Old Testament through the prophet, Malachi:

> See, I will send you the prophet Elijah before that great and dreadful day of the LORD comes.
>
> He will turn the hearts of the fathers to their children, and the hearts of the children to their fathers; or else I will come and strike the land with a curse. (Malachi 4:5-6)

Absent or uncaring fathers contribute to major social problems today—especially crime and homosexuality.

Understanding Men's Dilemma

God hasn't changed His mind about the place of men in the family and in society, and the enemy hasn't stopped his warfare against them. On today's spiritual and social battlefields Satan continues to target manhood in his quest for the destruction of the family. So if a wife takes her God-given role of helper to her husband, together they can soar above the enemy's plan.

The devil's attacks are obvious. Look at them. The wars of this century robbed our country of three generations of potential leaders by killing and crippling many of our finest young men. When they returned home after suffering the personal impact of war, they found home life greatly changed. Wives and children had been getting along without them, sometimes better than when they were there. Re-establishing their authority in the family was difficult.

Furthermore, the feminist agenda, affirmative action, the welfare system, and the evils of pornography have since combined to rob manhood of its character. There's more, but this will give some sense of the source of the problem. While they need to be accountable, blaming men will not help; recognizing and supporting them will.

A Wife's Support

A wife is under her husband to support him, not to be a weight to him. And in that role she is to be protected, not to be trampled on. Husband and wife support and protection works both ways. They support each other in common endeavors, and protect each other from outside influences. This especially applies to the intimate part of the relationship where no one else invades.

In this context the sexual needs of each partner in a marriage is to be addressed. God's Word makes it very clear that He expects loving consideration from each one for the other's feelings. The physical union of man and wife is a sacred act ordained by God for the consummation of the marriage toward a promised family unit. Its purpose is not only for the perpetuation of the human race through children but for a fulfillment of the deep need for intimacy.

While it's a physical union in which two become one, it's also a spiritual union like no other experience known to mankind. God, who is a Spirit, gives us Christ the bridegroom and the Church His bride as evidence of this deliberate design. Fidelity to the sexual relationship then takes on a spiritual dimension. The Apostle Paul wrote:

> But since there is so much immorality, each man should have his own wife, and each woman her own husband.
>
> The husband should fulfill his marital duty to his wife, and likewise the wife to her husband.
>
> The wife's body does not belong to her alone but also to her husband. In the same way, the husband's body does not belong to him alone but also to his wife.
>
> Do not deprive each other except by mutual consent and for a time, so that you may devote yourselves to prayer. Then come together again so that Satan will not tempt you because of your lack of self-control.   (1 Corinthians 7:2-5)

This is 'love giving' rather than 'love making.' Loving response to a mate's need fulfills both wife and husband. Conflicts of the day that have not been resolved before bedtime will drive a wedge between a couple and spoil the needed intimacy. So we see that Paul's admonition in Ephesians 4:26, "Do not let the sun go down while you are still angry," is wise counsel. Truly, "love covers over a multitude of sins" (1 Peter 4:8). A loving submissive heart will find it easier to obey.

There's no place here for withholding sexual favors to get something else you want; neither is there a place for insisting on favors while ignoring your partner's need. And there is need. God put in us a sexual drive that is dangerous if not met by the marriage partner.

Each one has a right, by way of the marriage commitment, to expect that the other will fill that need. Nature and her emotions dictate that it is the woman who submits. In Colossians 3:18, the Apostle Paul directs the wife to "submit to your husbands, as is fitting in the Lord." Although there is sometimes debate about Paul's reasons for giving such directions, it is nothing more than a restatement of the male dominance that God established from the beginning.

Man's Dominion Over The Earth

When God created Adam He put him in the garden to tend it. All went well until Satan tempted Eve. She yielded to the temptation, disobeyed God and influenced Adam to do the same. The nature of mankind then fell from a state of purity and fellowship with God to one of depravity and separation from Him. God had told Adam to have dominion over the earth and subdue it (Genesis 1:26-28). After the fall, part of his punishment was to earn his bread by the sweat of his brow, but most of his dominion was not taken away.

Man was created to have a dominion and dependence relationship with the earth that would be worked out by his own efforts. Often, however, his work in today's world fails to provide the opportunity to exercise dominion. That's why recreational activities and home ownership are important to him. Yet, he is not complete without the woman who was made to compliment him in his efforts and share dominion with him.

When a Man is Absent or Disabled

When man for some reason cannot or will not serve as the leader, God will use a woman and bless her. She must be careful, however, not to usurp a man's God-given authority. There are some situations in life in which it's necessary to lean hard on God's wisdom, and this is one of them. God has promised wisdom to those who ask, so His promise of help is there. "If any of you lacks wisdom, he should ask God, who gives generously to all without finding fault, and it will be given to him" (James 1:5).

If a man's physical or emotional condition makes him unable to lead, his wife's stepping into leadership makes him no less a man, and no less God's head of the family. So when a wife must, of necessity, lead in matters of home activities and decisions, she must be careful to keep an attitude toward him that respects and preserves his manhood and leadership position.

While a woman's basic emotional need is to be loved, a husband's basic need is to be respected. The Bible says, "each one of you also must love his wife as he loves himself, and the wife must respect her husband" (Ephesians 5:33). This rule applies even when she needs to take charge of things. She needs to apologize to no one for her role of leadership, but she must always keep in mind that it's a role of necessity and not the ideal one.

The marriage vows to love and honor in sickness and in health are for this kind of situation. The extra love required to live it, however, is seldom considered before the wedding. Since love is a choice, the hard places prove the level of commitment, through submission to the need. Life becomes richer as you go through the hard places together with the Lord.

Help For The Hard Places

God has a plan for help from other members of the body of Christ. Paul's instruction to Titus reveals God's intention that older women should instruct younger women:

>   You must teach what is in accord with sound
> doctrine.
>
>   Teach the older men to be temperate, worthy of
> respect, self-controlled, and sound in faith, in love
> and in endurance.
>
>   Likewise, teach the older women to be reverent
> in the way they live, not to be slanderers or addicted
> to much wine, but to teach what is good.
>
>   Then they can train the younger women to love
> their husbands and children,
>
>   to be self-controlled and pure, to be busy at home,
> to be kind, and to be subject to their husbands, so that
> no one will malign the word of God.   (Titus 2:1-5)

Many of our older women have much to teach. They
are an often untapped resource for helping families cope
with difficulties. To a younger woman who desires her
help, an older woman could be a God-send—a mother-
figure, if you will. For instance, the concept of
submission has been so skewed that a practical approach
is hard to find. However, these older women can be the
best help as they share lessons learned through experience
and during their younger years.

There are other issues that may be benefited as well
from hearing the voice of experience, such as the unequal
yoke. When people are young and blindly in love they
are often opposed to God's Word against it—which will
usually result in great harm to them unless someone can
show them by experience that it is always better to go
God's way.

The Unequal Yoke

The Apostle Paul admonishes us not to be unequally yoked with an unbeliever. In other words, a saved person is not to marry an unsaved person. While that is true, a closer look also takes into account the depth of commitment to the Lord, whether much or little.

A person whose heart is fully surrendered to the Savior will be frustrated when he or she is tied to a person who settles for less. Conversely, the uncommitted person will have little understanding of the deepest concerns and life purpose of their committed spouse and will be frustrated because of it. This lack of understanding can easily develop into jealousy over the love relationship their spouse has with the Lord and put a strain on the marriage.

Since marriage ties two people in all that they are and do, this becomes an additional unequal yoke that frustrates both parties. It is in this type of unequal relationship that the wife or husband who holds the deeper commitment to Christ must be submitted to God and be obedient in patient, understanding love. What better place to prove love and loyalty to Christ than in the crucible of daily experience.

Our first duty to people is to the lifetime vows that were made before God at the wedding altar. The most important earthly relationship we have is to our marriage partner, and we must learn to live out that relationship in love and righteousness. Without that, any other service to God is hindered.

> Husbands, in the same way be considerate as you
> live with your wives, and treat them with respect as
> the weaker partner and as heirs with you of the
> gracious gift of life, so that nothing will hinder your
> prayers.   (1 Peter 3:7)

When a husband and wife are both committed to loving God, they have the basis for true spiritual unity as well as the union of marriage bonds. The Bible says, "Do two walk together unless they have agreed to do so?" (Amos 3:3). The agreement that brings true unity is love for God—this binds people together and enhances all other relationships.

Regarding Biblical womanhood, Dorothy Patterson writes, "True femininity . . . is a glad affirmation of worthy masculine leadership."[1]

As we get back to the design God gave for marriage, home life can again become the nurturing secure place it was intended to be. There's no need to sacrifice anything good of the real 'gains' women have made. "no good thing does he withhold from those whose walk is blameless" (Psalm 84:11). That includes women!

Paul's direction on wifely submission is preceded by instruction to all Christians to be submitted to one another. He then said to husbands, "love your wives, just as Christ loved the church and gave himself up for her" (Ephesians 5:25).

Christ loved—and He gave himself. This is the quality of love that God's word says a man should have for his wife.

What wife wouldn't count it joy to be in submission to a husband whose heart was filled with that quality of love for her? The Biblical perspective on marriage isn't 'old fashioned' as some may think. It's eternal!

[1] "Recovering Biblical Manhood and Womanhood" by Ray Ortlund, Wayne Grudem, and Dorothy Patterson. (© Copyrighted August 1992, *Family Voice Magazine*, Published by Concerned Women For America, Washington, D.C.)

****7****

In Defense of Strong Women

From Submission to Leadership

In the words of a male friend of mine, "Submission is a woman's issue. Men don't need to understand it." That thinking is a carry-over from the past when women were basically thought of as subservient, simply because they were women. The Bible seems to support that view. Life has opened new vistas for women, however, and with them the need to re-think what God's Word really says to this issue.

First of all, submission is not gender-specific, except on the issue of marriage. Ephesians 5:22 says that a wife is to be in submission to her *own* husband—that is, not to other men. On the subject of teaching, Paul said, "I do not permit a woman to teach or to have authority over a man; she must be silent" (1 Timothy 2:12). Please note, this is Paul's advice to Church leaders for his day.

For nearly two thousand years the social and economic mores made that a wise position for the church. Many who converted to Christianity came out of pagan worship where many of their gods were female. Man was created in God's own image, and Eve was an extension of the creation of man. Because of His unique relationship to man in creation, it would have been in God's wisdom to keep the concept of leadership restricted to men. In this way He discouraged the tendency to return to idolatry.

Masculine leadership is still His best plan. A woman's highest calling was, and still is, to take care of the family. But in God's time, with the latter rain outpouring of the Holy Spirit in this century, came women's empowerment in spiritual things. It was time for Galatians 3:28 to become a reality: "There is neither Jew nor Greek, slave nor free, male nor female, for you are all one in Christ Jesus." What other explanation can you give to reconcile the reality of the Holy Spirit's work during this century with Paul's instructions to Timothy?

At the beginning of what may be the final century for spreading the gospel, the Holy Spirit began, with the Pentecostal outpouring, to work through women equally with men. In the history of the Azusa Street revival is recorded the breakdown of walls between gender, races, and socioeconomic levels.

Concurrent with women being included in the forefront of the spiritual world, the secular world also began giving them recognition and opportunities previously reserved for men. They have been given equality with men on increasing levels. In the Holy Spirit revival, God was ahead of the game. He had already opened the spiritual door to prepare women for the path they would take in the secular world.

The first person to receive the baptism of the Holy Spirit with speaking in tongues was a woman, Agnes N. Ozman, in a Bible School in Wichita, Kansas. Not coincidentally, it happened on January 1, 1901, the first day of the this century. Then in 1906, a woman pastor of a Nazarene church in Los Angeles, a Reverend Mrs. Hutchinson, invited a black minister, Tom Seymour, to preach at her church. Later that year, from an abandoned old building on Azusa Street that had been used variously as a Methodist church, a stable, and a warehouse, God used Tom Seymour to spearhead a world-changing Pentecostal revival. For three glorious years the Holy Spirit touched, without discrimination, all who came to the Azusa Street church. All received the same power, and were commissioned by the Holy Spirit to spread the fire.

Out of that revival many women were called and anointed by the Holy Spirit into places of leadership. Amy Semple McPherson is an early example. During the Twenties, she led the miracle revival that established the Foursquare Church. It still remains doctrinally true to its roots. A generation later Kathryn Kuhlman was raised up with a healing ministry that honored the power of the Holy Ghost. Currently, Marilyn Hickey and Kay Arthur are each powerful teachers on a world wide scale.

Not to be overlooked is the fact that ninety per cent of the home cell groups that are the driving force in the 750,000 member Assembly of God Church in Seoul, Korea, are headed by women. The underground house churches in mainline China are also mostly headed by women.

There have been a host of other women called by the Lord into leadership during this century. Beverly LaHaye, founder of Concerned Women for America and Mother Theresa of Calcutta, India, fame are two who come to mind. I'm sure you can think of some who have blessed your life.

I said all that to say this: When God does something, who are we to reject it? Obviously, God intends a place for women in spiritual leadership.

In spite of that evidence, much of the Church has either kept, or has resorted to, the attitude that prevailed in Paul's day. Perhaps we can discover why.

Reasons to Reject Leadership of Women

The reason Paul gave was that Eve was deceived but Adam was not. It sounds like a woman isn't to be trusted. Paul must have seen something in her nature that makes her vulnerable to Satan's wiles. Is it that she was made to have more emotional and spiritual sensitivity than a man and thus prone to deception?

Does that capacity also give her a sensitivity to the Holy Spirit in a way special to women? If so, when it's surrendered to the Holy Spirit, it should become a blessing. That in her which is dangerous in the natural may be an asset in the hands of the Holy Spirit.

Perhaps the reason Paul took the position he did is that the potential dangers without the Holy Spirit in charge are not to be ignored. His teaching may have been a needed safeguard until the time of the latter rain outpouring. Those who do not entertain the presence and power of the Holy Spirit are still, regardless of doctrine, often blinded to the place of women in leadership.

Clearly, God's best choice is that leadership be in the hands of men. Consequently the usefulness of women will depend on masculine acceptance of them. "Unfair," you say? Perhaps so, from our limited, temporal, perspective. God's ways, however, are eternal. He doesn't operate on "women's rights" language of today, and He always makes it come out right in the long run. Ladies, stay in submission to God's will and be on standby for when He needs you.

Keep in mind that when men fail to adequately represent Him, it seems that God turns to women to fill the void. His work will be done, and He will use vessels available to Him. Remember, also, that there is a dimension of ministry that needs the special touch of a woman. Look for it.

It's now a proven fact that men and women have different brain function. Amazing, isn't it? God knew that all along. The characteristics that make a woman think and feel differently from a man gives her a capacity for ministering from a woman's point of view. With the blending of men and women's issues today, that view is needed.

The Strong Christian Woman in Her Own World

So far, I have talked only about women in ministry, and you may say, "I don't relate to that." Perhaps not, but to know God approves gives room for affirmation of your own vision—or clarifies your opinion of others. Whatever your lot in life, there's a place for a woman who holds in her heart a vision and a purpose.

"Find a need and fill it, find a hurt and heal it," is a motto for doing God's work wherever you are. As you submit to the needs of others, some will be inspired to go with you. Be ready to take leadership, but keep in mind there's a price. Leadership requires that you submit to the responsibility of authority.

As a part of that responsibility, be prepared to deal with your own need to develop a meek and quiet spirit, which is of great value to God (1 Peter 3:4). When you live in meekness, the strength within you is like a well trained horse under harness. Instead of dangerously running wild, you are able to live in intelligent self control. Since meekness and self control are both elements of the fruit of the Holy Spirit (Galatians 5:22-23), you have supernatural help.

Rather than the weakness it's often purported to be, meekness is a strength that provides the ability to release painful relationship issues to God's hand without the need to keep score. Forgiving others for wrongs you have suffered thus becomes easier and in turn releases you to spiritual health and effectiveness. Try it at work, in PTA, or anywhere you have influence. God calls His women to be salt and light to the world—the *best* salt and light.

To Serve Others

Are you, for whatever reason, finding problems in dealing with people? If so, a simple key to help you handle difficult relationships is to seek solutions by asking questions rather than making declarations. That approach serves rather than gives commands. It puts you in a place to make people feel understood, even though you may not agree with them. When they feel their opinion has value, they are more likely to listen to yours. It's an expression of a submissive heart and a skill worth developing.

All facets of leadership work on the same principle. Whether in the family, the church, on the job, or working on a community project, a woman in leadership must be able to inspire others to share in her vision and purpose.

If she has chosen to devote her life to home and hearth, this is the woman whose family life is her field of ministry. In her mature years she becomes the matriarch of her clan and leaves an imprint on her world through her children and her influence on the community. She inspires her husband and molds her children's lives for eternity. Among modern women, Barbara Bush is a good example.

Drawing from another era, my grandmother was such a woman. She lived during the first part of this century, before the industrial revolution took shape. She was an Ozark pioneer wife, a mother of nine, and the neighborhood health care giver. Not because of formal training or for money, but because of her willingness to give of what she had to those who were in need.

Our definition of submission in chapter two was, "Accepting the other persons definition of your relationship". Although Grandma would not have called it submission, our definition applies. She accepted the needs she found among family and neighbors as defining her place in relationship to the community.

The Strong Woman as a Wife

As a strong woman in the Nineties, you must understand your role of submission to your husband. So much of living draws you away from God's order for your home that it's sometimes difficult to find your way back. His blessing is upon those who strive to find and live in His plan. If a husband is ready to take leadership, a wife's job is clear—thank God for him and submit to being the helper God intended you to be.

But what do you do about the husband who doesn't want leadership, or even headship? In the minds of observers who are not in that situation, you have no defense when in their eyes they see you as an aggressive woman with a henpecked husband. You need to ask, "Does leadership come from choice, from ability, or is it naturally a part of the male condition?

In the minds of many wives, being married to a passive man when your goal is to submit to a strong leader-husband is frustrating. You may resent that you have to take responsibility for things you thought were his to do and make decisions for which you are not prepared. But if he isn't taking charge, somebody has to do it. Your family cannot stumble through life without leadership.

If you have to take a leadership role, your husband might be intimidated by your self-assurance and apparent superior ability. There are many possible explanations for his behavior, but here's one: he may be remembering all the females who seemed to be superior to him as he was growing up. For instance, he may have seen his father take a recessive attitude in the home, so his mother ran things—perhaps even his father. In addition, his teachers were usually women. Then there were all those girls in school who were smarter than the boys because of developmental differences.

He may be feeling the same futility he felt then and is reacting to it in the way that worked for him as a boy. Rather than fight for a place in a battle he felt he could not win, he learned to take a passive approach and let others concern themselves with leadership. A strong wife easily becomes the 'others.' And yet, your husband chose you because your type of personality easily fit his perspective of marriage.

If that scenario describes your situation, there's hope. Love your husband just as he is, work at understanding him, and support in him what you want to encourage. Criticism won't accomplish much, so don't do it. Take leadership in things he asks you to without apology. It may not seem so, but that's submission.

Opposites Attract

Quite often the qualities that attract people to each other become the very ones that drive them apart. A case in point is when a wife's assertive nature overrides the passive nature of her husband. While these opposite characteristics are appealing at first, the place of dominance eventually becomes a thorny issue. Many a woman struggles with self-condemnation because of the failure to resolve this issue.

Marriage takes the cooperation of both parties, so if her husband does not conform to her idea of his role as leader, she reasons, "What am I doing wrong?" or, "How can I change him?" She cannot change him. The only person she can change is herself and her own thinking. The difference it makes in her, may or may not entice him to change.

If she sees herself at fault for being in a position of leadership, or if he openly resents her ability in this regard, then a nagging guilt develops and holds her captive. If she sees herself as not at fault, yet considers her position of leadership to be a fault in her marriage,

91

she'll more than likely blame any ensuing problems on her husband, thereby widening the gap between them and devastating the relationship.

Often she'll see her choices to be between drawing into a shell and hiding her potential behind his inadequacy, or pursuing a separate course that will destroy the quality of the marriage relationship. Both are unacceptable. There has to be another way. A marriage is in trouble not when the break-up is near, but when the thinking begins to be directed independently rather than in unity—when it becomes more "I" then "we".

If you value your marriage more than your own ambitions, you have a good chance of coming to terms with the things that would pull you apart. Starting over again without him is not what it may appear from your view inside the safety of a marriage. If the choice is yours, don't throw it away lightly. Vows before God don't erase.

I was married for thirty-three years to a wonderful man who resisted leadership. My ideal was for him to be the strong head of the home I knew he was capable of being, and what I was raised with. Nothing I could do, however, would change him. I finally settled for being thankful to God for the goodness I enjoyed, and loving him right where he was. I could admire his stability, faithfulness, gentleness, physical strength, his wisdom and love for God. Not bad, don't you agree?

It took me too long to reach that place but I was glad the Lord guided me to it. At one point in my marriage I was chaffing under the demands of my husband's need as it kept my activities restricted. Then the Lord shined a spotlight on my need for an attitude change. As I submitted to God in my circumstances, I was able to say, "Lord, if you love this man so much as to give my life completely to his need, who am I to complain?" It was a point of reaffirming my sense of servanthood to the Savior, and became a renewal of joy in my love for my husband.

Just as Adam needed Eve, your husband, whether or not he accepts headship, needs a wife who will complete him and bring out the best in him. It's up to you to adjust to what he needs from you. In so doing you'll be putting your family on a firm foundation of love.

The family that is living in God's order is being attacked as never before because it is the bulwark of all that's good. Satan knows his kingdom cannot prevail against God's people so long as the family is in order and is led by the Spirit of God.

If ever there was a time and place for a strong woman to assert herself in righteousness on all levels, this is the place, and this is the time. We need women who will hold a high standard of integrity wherever their influence reaches, at work, in the Church, or in the home; women who will take leadership alongside men in the fight for the survival of the family; women who make their lives count for eternity.

No apologies are needed for a godly woman with leadership qualities. Let's thank God for the talents He's given us and put them to good use.

****8****

Living Examples

Our Story

In my marriage I've handled submission both the right way and the wrong way. I'm convinced that my husband, David, was a man born to greatness. God gave him all the attributes usually found in a man who is a leader. But because he was painfully conscientious about responsibility and lacking in self-confidence, he was reluctant to take leadership. As a result, there were many times when I was groping in the dark to learn how to be the godly wife I desired to be, to follow the submission message I found in my Bible, and to still be true to the real life needs of myself and my family.

While David was a very conscientious provider for us, his desire for me was that I be capable of financial independence. He needed me to take much of the responsibility for all the working details of our business and social affairs that were troublesome to him.

Other than providing for the family and taking care of outside things, he saw his role as supportive of all I wanted to do, and in that way he felt he was being really good to me. This was a pattern that had been laid down by his father before him.

The home in which I was raised was run by a very different set of rules. My father lived an exemplary life but was quite autocratic in the details of family activities with little choices left for my mother, except in the way she handled the farm/home work load and the care of five children. Nevertheless, she managed to find a way to make it fulfilling for herself and instill healthy attitudes in her children.

My husband and I spent thirty plus years working out the difference in our expectations of each other, according to the opposite role models of our parents. We had much in common with regard to our family values, however, and because of our faith in God we survived the rough times.

For years I struggled against my resentment of his failure to be the strong leader I wanted to follow. The Lord brought victory when I finally reached the point of being able to freely love him for the good man that he was—and there was plenty of good in him to love—without any sense of resentment that he could not be what I felt I needed him to be.

I learned to trust that God knew what He was doing for us both when He brought us together. To be at my best, I needed the freedom he gave me—and the approval he so generously offered. I also came to realize that there were things in me that were difficult for David to deal with, and yet he patiently endured with hardly a complaint.

It took many years of marriage for me to develop this attitude, but during the last year or so of David's life it gave me more peace and enjoyment than I had ever known, and I'm so thankful for it. I only regret I was so long in reaching that place of inner and outer harmony.

Submission Rewarded—Children

One precious memory I have of our life together demonstrates the value of following a husband's leadership. After twelve years of marriage, my first pregnancy was an answer to a prayer of commitment. I finally asked God for a baby on condition that I have absolute assurance that the child would spend eternity in heaven with me. I promised to do my best to raise him to please the Lord.

God answered that prayer with a most delightful baby boy. All his life Bryan has been a son to be proud of and a testimony of God's abundant blessing. No further children came to join him, however, and one day when he was four years old he told me that he had been praying for a little boy to play with.

Actually, his prayer was answered within a few months when new neighbors moved in with a son his age. I assumed, however, that he had meant a little brother, and since we wanted another child while he was young, we began giving serious consideration to adoption.

I was convinced we should pursue it. David wasn't so sure. During this period in our lives, he was reading the Bible aloud to me almost every evening while I washed the dishes. He had completed the New Testament twice and was reading a third version, when he came to the passage where Jesus said, "And whoever welcomes a little child like this in my name welcomes me" (Matthew 18:5).

We both felt the impact of those words. He stopped reading, I stopped in the middle of washing a plate, and we looked at each other. David said, "I think that's our answer."

The next day we phoned the county adoption agency and began the process of qualifying through them for one of the many babies available at that time. We expected our application would be processed rapidly. Four days later, however, a television half-hour special was aired about the need for adoptive parents for children of all ages, even newborns.

This made the community aware of the availability of children and the ease of qualifying, and there quickly followed a flood of applications from want-to-be adoptive parents. As a result, it became increasingly difficult to be accepted, so we waited.

We had two things against us—we had one natural child, and we were older than most applicants. It was because of our age that our application was rejected eight months after we applied. There were plenty of younger applicants.

I was devastated by the rejection. I had been so sure that we were obeying God's Word to us and for months had felt my heart preparing for a new baby, almost like it had been while I waited for our son to be born.

Many questions remained unanswered. Why had God brought us this far if the answer was to be "no". What do we do now with the Scripture He had quickened to our hearts? Where do we go next to find a baby?

During prayer, I received a promise from the Lord for our baby. "Wait for the LORD; be strong and take heart and wait for the LORD" (Psalm 27:14). My heart was at peace—I would wait.

There followed months of wondering just when God would fulfill His promise. Nothing seemed to be happening. Time and again I suggested to my husband ways in which we could help God to find a baby for us.

David's reply was always the same: "When the Lord has our baby it will come to us without our doing anything about it. God said wait, and that's what we will do." More waiting. Finally, because I trusted David's sense of God's will, I gave in to his firm stand and dropped the subject, even in my own mind.

Two and a half years later the phone rang one day and a friend who had helped us in the past asked, "Are you still looking for a baby? There's one available."

My heart skipped a beat and I said, "I can't answer for sure until I talk to David. Don't contact anyone else until you hear from me."

When I asked him there wasn't even the hint of a hesitation. "Of course we want it. That's the baby the Lord has for us". He intuitively knew this was to be a girl and always referred to her by name, Heather LeAnne. For him a boy's name was out of the question.

Six weeks later we held in our arms the sweetest, tiniest little bundle of joy we could imagine. She was really ours. All five pounds and three ounces of her, and just eighteen inches long. She was smaller than a lot of dolls, but perfectly healthy and all ours. Her childhood was a joy to us as well, and she has grown up to be a beautiful young woman. I feel privileged to be her mother.

My submission to David's leadership in this matter resulted in our having a lovely daughter of God's choice and in His time instead of mine. Because God gave her to us, she greatly enriched our lives and is a real source of strength and joy to me now that I'm a widow.

The assurance that God's gift was given in His perfect time and thus brought to us the right child, has been a help in trusting Him to see us through the hard times without David. Being a single parent wasn't easy, but Heather's presence and love continues to help give meaning and focus to my life. Submitting to my husband's leadership paid big dividends during our life together and continues to do so.

Failure to Submit - the Penalty

An example of a wrong submission action on my part occurred during the last year David and I had together. I decided we needed a swimming pool but David objected to it. I insisted and he finally conceded when I assured him I would pay for it out of my earnings.

I was sure our children would benefit from having our own pool to share with their friends. In addition I felt confident that I could persuade David to get some needed exercise and perhaps prolong his life. He was on disability retirement at the time because of a heart condition. I convinced myself that these were good and logical reasons and justified our spending the money for the pool. Even so, David said he would never use it.

How right he was.

He died before it was completed.

Then Bryan moved out in preparation for marriage and Heather doesn't like to swim alone.

Since I'm not a swimmer, the main effect of the pool was the ongoing work and expense of upkeep, and a beautiful spot to look at in the back yard. Certainly not sufficient reason to keep it and so I had it removed—an extra expense and needless work I could have been spared had I listened to my husband and followed his leadership.

Misguided Submission

At one important point in David's life I failed him miserably. It was after he retired and had received a small settlement for damage to his hearing from a lifetime of working with jet engines. His hope was that the amount he received could be used buy a truck for post-retirement use. He was particular about its quality and looks.

A friend directed him to one that seemed just right. I left the decision entirely to him, feeling that in order to be the submissive wife, I needed to let him make the decisions. So I didn't take responsibility to share with him my evaluation of the truck purchase. How wrong I was not to.

That transaction was the devil's own mischief. The only good thing about that vehicle was its looks. It had probably been driven well over 100,000 miles but only showed 18,000 on the odometer. The truck had also been wrecked and then cleverly repaired just enough to hide the problems and give it an almost new appearance.

David was no novice at mechanics but he didn't see it, neither did our friend who gave the okay, until it was too late. After paying a good price to buy that truck, we spent enough in repairs to have bought a new one and then lost money trading it for a car.

Had I been responsive to his need for me to be thinking clearly on the issue I perhaps could have saved him from that heartache and disappointment. We both were seduced through David's desire to buy a truck and his friend's desire to help him, and I failed to explore with him the possibility of fraud.

101

He was asking for my help and would have listened to me, but I did not give him the support he needed to avoid Satan's snare. Instead of being the helper to him that God intended me to be, I was—at that time—still not clear about it. I was reluctant to take any initiative from my husband, and tried to be a 'submissive wife' according to the conventional spiritual wisdom of that day.

I remember feeling frustrated and helpless during the truck transaction, hoping it would turn out all right. I was still struggling with the whole concept of not sharing in any decision-making and so forcing my husband to be the sole decider as head of the home. I now see headship differently—not as a matter of decision making but one of taking responsibility, which David did well. But a responsible husband deserves and needs his wife's best opinion and support in decisions that affect them both. She shares in the results and needs to share in the responsibility for decision making. This is mutual submission.

Our truck purchase was an example of submission that kills rather than contributes to life. Had I helped my husband come to a decision that would have avoided the problem, and he went against it, responsibility for the results would have been his. I would have needed to accept it without rancor, releasing it to him. Had I concurred in the wrong decision, it would have meant sharing equally in responsibility for the results. Whatever might have happened, at least we both would have done our best together.

I could give more examples from my own experience that would attest to the value of following a husband's leadership in all the ways you can trust it. But even where you don't have confidence in the decision he's making, you should weigh carefully any venture outside God's obviously prescribed pattern.

Your husband or wife is your first field of ministry. God wants to love you both through each other.

Queen Esther - Authority and Submission

In the Old Testament book of Esther, we have a beautiful story of a Jewish orphan girl who became Queen of the Persian Empire. At that time King Ahasuerus ruled all the known world. The story is full of excitement, suspense and intrigue, and ends with an assurance that all is well in God's world and with His people.

Esther was submissive and obedient to her cousin Mordecai who had raised her as his daughter, and because of her beauty, both physical and spiritual, she was accepted by King Ahasuerus as his wife. Esther replaced Vashti who was banished because of her refusal to obey his command to come before his companions so he could display her beauty.

Esther, as queen later saved the Jews from extinction by risking her life in appearing uninvited before the king. He was enthralled by her beauty and by her attitude toward him and received her.

In spite of the gravity of the situation Esther did not immediately ask the king for anything but rather appealed to his curiosity and social nature. She must have made a study of him and knew how he would react. She planned a special dinner for the following day to which she invited him and Haman, the originator of the treacherous plot.

The king was unaware of its implications or the fact that she was Jewish. However, when Mordecai, her cousin, revealed to Esther Haman's sinister plot to destroy the whole Jewish race, he told her of a situation that the king could not see. She then appealed to the king according to the weapons at her disposal. These were her beauty, her wit and wisdom in her relationship to the king, and the support of family and friends who joined her in fasting and prayer.

She submitted to the king because of a higher submission to her uncle Mordecai, who is a type of the Holy Spirit. She was willing to lay her life down if necessary for the work to which she was called. Her submission meant to risk her life for the life of her people.

Because Esther submitted according to God's plan, she was victorious over Haman, who would have destroyed her and her people. Instead, she saw the complete destruction of the enemy and vindication of her people as they were given a place of honor throughout the land at the command of the king.

Esther is a beautiful example of the wisdom of first submitting to the Holy Spirit, then to your husband, and watch God work.

Abigail and Her Evil Husband

Abigail was a woman who knew how to handle a marriage to a cruel and ungodly man, Nabal. Read about it in 1 Samuel, Chapter 25. She did not allow his actions to cause her to become bitter and evil, either by joining in his way of living, or by allowing herself to become so taken up in resisting that she became blinded to her responsibilities to others.

In full recognition of his evil ways and without justifying him, she took it upon herself to cover for him for the sake of her household, and prevailed upon David not to take vengeance on them. Her eventual reward was that she was set free by Nabal's death, and later became the wife of King David.

The King of kings still rewards those who are faithful to him, even in a bad marriage. The Bridegroom of the Church promises to fill empty places and to supply all your needs. Relationship to Him is the answer.

In evaluating these examples of headship and submission, we have a variety of situations and personalities. Through them all, one truth shines through: God's way is best, no matter the circumstances or the situations. He is Lord of circumstances and situations and His truth is bigger than any man's interpretation.

His way will always be right for you.

9

Submission of Parents and Obedience of Children

The Family—A Sacred Trust

All authority brings responsibility with it. The authority parents hold over children is a sacred trust like no other. Submitting to the responsibility for training and discipline of their children distinguishes good parents from bad ones. The reason for the difference you see between well behaved children and those who are allowed to run amok is usually found in the willingness or unwillingness of parents to accept the responsibility for obedience training.

The Bible instructs children to obey and to honor their parents, but they can't do that without parental training. The responsibility thus rests squarely on the shoulders of parents to exercise their God-given authority in a way that gets results. But without help, it isn't easy to find the way.

Good parenting is difficult and puzzling at best. Changes in our society during the last three or four generations give little or no precedent for many of today's challenges. Child psychologists not withstanding, trial and error is often the mode, and if the trial turns into error it's too late to fix it. There is no second chance in raising children.

The book, Future Shock, by Alvin Toffler[1] highlights the problem of our inability to deal with a culture that changes at such a dizzying pace that people lose contact with any stabilizing roots. The problem clearly applies to raising children and understanding how they relate to their fast changing world. Often their situations are new to us, and we have to handle them without the benefit of experience to guide us.

Christians must go back to the basics and bring back time honored practices of child training—those that have their roots in instructions from God's Word. Ephesians 6:1 says, "Children, obey your parents in the Lord, for this is right." Thus our scriptural foundation for child raising is obedience training and teaching them to respect authority.

The command to children is followed by the one to parents, particularly fathers, to understand the child and teach him, feeding his spirit according to the love nature of God. "Fathers, do not provoke *or* irritate *or* fret your children—do not be hard on them or harass them; lest they become discouraged *and* sullen *and* morose *and* feel inferior *and* frustrated; do not break their spirit" (Colossians 3:21, AMP).

Obedience Training

Obedience training is best begun very early. When a baby begins to resist diaper changing is a good time to let him know you love him but you're in charge. Gentle but firm discipline will prepare him for the next phase.

The exploring toddler needs very specific guidance and control. This is the time when a necessary spanking can be the best and most loving way to impress him. A light but definite swat on his diaper or bare leg, along with a firm tone of voice, can do wonders to get his attention. It's the easiest and most effective kind of training discipline for him to understand and respond to—and keeps him from far harder and more painful discipline later in life.

A simple, clear, command allows the child to assimilate what is expected of him before going on, so as not to frustrate and confuse him. A small child cannot process too many things at one time, but even he needs to be held accountable by follow-through.

As he grows, he will be ready for the next stage with a minimum of problems—less spankings needed and more response to reasoning. By the age of six, spankings should be pretty much behind him—no pun intended. At this stage, other means of training should take the place of spankings, except as a response reinforcement in those cases of extreme rebellion, which should be few.

The object is to train in obedience, keeping in mind the characteristics of each child. There will of necessity be some sort of discomfort, since that's what gets his attention for an attitude change. The Bible tells us that even Jesus learned obedience by the things He suffered (Hebrews 5:8). Since He had no sin for which to be corrected, it means He learned the sometimes painful cost of obedience. A child can relate to Him in that way.

Time To Listen

As you teach obedience to your children, keep communication open, especially from six or seven years on. Lots of listening will pay big dividends later during the adolescent and teen years when they are ready to strike out on their own and break from dependence on you. If you don't want to listen to childhood patter at this stage, you're not likely to get the opportunity to hear what they have to say or have them listen to you later on. At that time, you'll desperately need to know what they're thinking and what's going on in their lives.

If you give your child the impression that what he has to say is a nuisance to you, that impression will be hard to change when he's more mature. Be aware of what's important to him, and respond to it even as you train him to be considerate of others. Often you may find it difficult to see any importance in what your child is highly concerned about, but remember you're both looking at the situation from different age and experience levels. To understand and help, you must look with your child's eyes and feelings, not your own. Only then can you properly and considerately guide from your age and experience level.

Things important to your child will help you decide where and how to release him appropriately. As he develops responsibility in things that interest him, you can judge his progress toward responsible independence. While a child is growing to independence from the parents, so are the parents from the child.

Tightly controlled parenting in the very early stage for the purpose of keeping the child from harm and yet teaching responsibility, lays a good foundation for confident releasing in the later years. Gradually releasing your child to being responsible for himself forestalls many problems and heartaches for both the parents and the child.

Often parents expect children to live the rules they have been taught without making room for the individuation process whereby they begin to understand and express their own individuality—it's a process that's essential to reaching healthy maturity. It's during this process that a young person throws off restraints to experience for himself where he stands and who he is apart from his parents, testing the values he has been taught and chosing to make them his own.

When that process is missing, often it's because unreasonable obedience was required that left no room for independence. There was no room either for other facets of training, such as the child's need to learn the principle behind the command and the reason God gave the principle. He will face life more like the child than an adult, and in later years it will catch up to him and cause many problems.

Lessons From the Word

You can avoid these pitfalls by making God's Word a practical part of every day, letting children see His love in action. The Israelites were instructed to teach God's Word throughout each day:

> These commandments that I give you today are to be upon your hearts.
>
> Impress them on your children. Talk about them when you sit at home and when you walk along the road, when you lie down and when you get up.
>
> (Deuteronomy 6:6-7)

That's God's plan still.

You're to talk with your children about the laws of God while you're sitting at home, when you walk about, when you go to bed and when you get up in the morning. Whatever you're doing, let them see God's place in it.

The goal is to build trust in God so that willing obedience and worship follows. And teach them thankfulness to God.

Let the child's own experiences build trust in God's love for him. A child needs to know that God relates to him and his young life every bit as much as He relates to an adult, but he will know it only as he is taught in a way that is appropriate for his age and maturity.

Faith comes naturally to a child and needs to be encouraged, even though it's a challenge to your own faith. Don't sell God short in the life of a child. He'll learn to develop his own relationship to God by what he sees, by what he hears, and by what he experiences much more than by formal teaching.

One hour at Sunday School is not enough and may, in the hands of a wrong teacher, do more harm than good. Many a child has grown up to reject the faith of childhood because of bad experiences connected with church training. Parents are often unaware, so stay on top of it. Be aware.

Out of The Nest

The teen years present a special challenge for keeping children out of harm's way. They need gradually to be allowed to try their wings and risk failure so that their own experiences will confirm what they've been taught, but yet controlled sufficiently so no permanent harm will come to them. Then is when the spiritual responsibility of parenting is limited to guiding children as they allow you to introduce them to a more mature relationship with God for themselves.

After you have done what you can, it's time to release them and change your relationship from one of authority over them to mutual submission, in which you will be receiving and giving support. They no longer are required to obey you, but rather to submit to you, just as you are to submit to them.

If your bird has left the nest with a broken wing, pray for God to do what you can't. Trust Him to bring healing and wholeness as only He can, in His will and in His time. It takes wisdom to know the difference between what you can and cannot do, and it takes patience, faith and hope to wait God's time to see results. It can be a painful process but that's what a maturing relationship is all about.

This process is an ever developing one from infancy to young adulthood. It is accomplished by a co-relationship between responsibility and privilege. The more responsible a child becomes, the more privilege he's allowed. The secret of success is in being willing to take the risk of releasing him, and having the wisdom to know the degree and time.

When a child is financially independent, ready to go on his own, or you have released him to independence, your relationship to him changes to one of mutual submission as to an adult. Your twenty-year assignment is changed. You never stop being a parent but you are freed up to do other things. You can enjoy the fruits of your labor in their lives.

Protecting Children From Abuse

There's another part of child training needed these days, as never before. Training children must of necessity include something of protection against dangers from predators, both friends and strangers. They must learn to be selective as to who or what they are to obey. The problem of child molestation is tragically not limited to the non-Christian world. Incest is a shocking reality in far too many 'Christian' homes, and there are many potential hazards in other situations.

This brings us to another issue: What of children who are being physically or sexually abused by a parent? Should they still be taught to obey?

If we could just look the other way and pretend this problem isn't there, we could avoid an unpleasant subject. Since the problem does indeed exist, however, a simplistic answer won't do. For every child who is so victimized, there's a perpetrator who also needs help, and there is God who loves them both. But He does have a special word of judgment for anyone who causes His little ones to fall.

The innocent child suffers, both in a damaged self image and in the loss of a healthy relationship with the perpetrator. The healing power of God is the only hope for a truly successful recovery. Often He uses counselors who understand the wounded spirit to minister His love and forgiveness. A good counselor is well worth whatever price is charged. A child's future is at stake.

What do you say to a child whose parent is alcoholic, abusive and cruelly demanding? Much of what has been taught says that the Bible teaches unquestioning submission to parents, trusting God to correct them. While there is something to be said for enduring hardship in the name of love, there's a line not to be crossed. The damage to the child from loss of family relationship should be balanced with the damage from continued abuse. It's not easy to determine the line of no return and save the child before he or she is forced across it.

My heart aches for a young person caught in such a situation and having no other counsel given to him or her except to obey parents because God will make it right. Honor and respect of parents does not require submission to sinful acts. Thankfully, any adult in a position of responsibility for a child who knows about such a situation in California, and in some other states, has a legal mandate to report it to the authorities.

When a child has the power to decide whether to stay or leave, it's dangerous, and often foolish, to counsel him to stay in order to please God. To have been in that kind of situation is already emotionally devastating. To believe that God requires him or her to stay and submit to it distorts the nature of God, especially His holiness and love.

If confidence in God is eroded, where will the child turn for healing? Especially the healing of damaged emotions. If 'Christian' people are part of the problem, where will he turn for the pure love so necessary for spiritual and emotional health? These questions need to be faced. A blanket approach to giving advice about problems with this kind of potential is most unwise.

The concept of submission was never intended to be used in this fashion. Neither was obedience. However it will be helpful, in sorting out the issues involved, to look at both to see how they fit our subject.

Obedience or Submission

Let's distinguish between obedience and submission. Obedience is what is done in response to a given command. That's the child's proper response to the parent. Submission is yielding to the authority of another person. It denotes taking responsibility and willingly fitting into a requirement.

115

You cannot command submission, so that's not properly a part of the child's relationship to the parents. A child is to obey commands. The relationship becomes submission when he is able to freely choose to submit out of love and honor.

Honor your parents, "that it may go well with you and that you may enjoy long life on the earth" (Ephesians 6:3), is a command from God to be obeyed. That means obedience to parents in the formative years, and holding them in high esteem in the adult years. If an adult cannot honor a parent's conduct, he can honor the place he or she held in God's plan for giving him life.

Learning obedience early is of vital importance because it fosters respect and lays the foundation for a pattern of obedience to our Heavenly Father, to whom we are always little children.

Adult Children At Home

A potential problem within the context of submission of children to parents is that of the older child. One who has a need to be in the same household as the parents but has reached an age of independence, both legally and financially. This situation is increasingly common these days and causes some distress when the roles are not clearly defined. The shadow from childhood frustrates the relationships.

Within the home, respect for parents is still important but it cannot take on the same characteristics that were there before. While the child is to respect the parent because of who the parent is in God's plan, and because home authority still belongs to its head, the parent must also respect the child's maturity and recognize his capability to handle his own affairs. When he is able to support himself, he should be released to live his own life, both as to privilege and responsibility. If he's living at home, the parents releasing him should be matched by his honoring them.

At this point the relationship of child to parents is changed from one of obedience to one of honor and mutual respect. If that's not possible because of sin, let him go, as did the father of the prodigal son (Luke 15:11-32). Perhaps even help him go, hardships notwithstanding. That may be what's needed to turn him around.

Parent-child submission, like all others is a two-way street. Parents submitting to the self-sacrifice necessary to be good parents—children submitting to obedience and honor because they have much to learn and because God says so.

God holds parents accountable for their parenting, and children for their honoring. But when a difficult situation arises, the standard for determining proper action is God's righteousness. It never contradicts the rest of His Word or His nature.

[1]*Future Shock* by Alvin Toffler (© Copyrighted 1970, Random House, NY)

10

Submission for Singles

Where Do Singles Belong?

In a Christian environment where God's Word is taken seriously, the subject of authority, submission and accountability will at some point come up. The Word is specific in instructions for marriage, church relationships, parents and children. It's not specific, however, as to how submission applies to the single adult. Consequently, the issue must be faced in the light of relationships within the body of Christ and the community.

Singles need a well defined spot to call their own. The singles ministries that have sprung up in recent years are meeting the need to a degree but are not the whole answer. Individual single people can serve the whole fellowship and need to be encouraged to do so.

In 1 Corinthians 7, the Apostle Paul gives his opinion of the necessity of being married, and the wisdom of staying unmarried. While encouraging marriage to be wholesome and good, he intersperses his opinion as to the desirability of remaining single. He makes his case for celibacy by saying that an unmarried person is free to totally give himself to God, whereas married people have an obligation to please one another. Sounds great, but will it work?

Paul does not elaborate on how relationships work for singles. Does that mean that you are left in limbo with no instructions? No, it means you are to bring your circumstances under the spotlight of the message given to the fellowship as a whole.

In a word, submit to God. Matthew 6:33 says, " But seek first his kingdom and his righteousness, and all these things will be given to you as well." Putting God first is what gives you a plan and a purpose in life. Let Him guide you through the details.

Perhaps the instructions on submission are obscure because everyone's situation is different, and so we need to rely on a principle. Let's explore the principle.

First, to whom does a single person submit? Here are some statements about that from the Word of God:

> Submit to one another out of reverence for Christ.
> (Ephesians 5:21)

> You know that the household of Stephanas were the first converts in Achaia, and they have devoted themselves to the service of the saints. I urge you, brothers, to submit to such as these, and to everyone who joins in the work, and labors at it.
>
> (1 Corinthians 16:15-16)

> Submit yourselves, then, to God. Resist the devil, and he will flee from you. (James 4:7)

Obey your leaders and submit to their authority. They keep watch over you as men who must give an account. Obey them so that their work will be a joy, not a burden, for that would be of no advantage to you.   (Hebrews 13:17)

Submit yourselves for the Lord's sake to every authority instituted among men: whether to the king, as the supreme authority, or to governors, who are sent by him to punish those who do wrong and to commend those who do right.   (1 Peter 2:13-14)

Young men, in the same way be submissive to those who are older. All of you, clothe yourselves with humility toward one another, because, "God opposes the proud but gives grace to the humble."
                                                          (1 Peter 5:5)

To summarize the meaning of these passages: you, along with all other Christians, are to submit to each other and to God. Your relationships will reflect the love of God that guides you as you practice submission in all your contacts with people.

Because you're single, you have more freedom to serve wholeheartedly in your chosen place. Hang loose on the issue of marriage and family. Understand it for others but know what you are about—serving God on a wider scale.

Singles—A Potential Powerhouse

There's much potential in the spiritual power within people who are given wholeheartedly to serve God.

Here's a list of possibilities for something to do that will make a difference:

> - Prayer is perhaps the most effective thing you can do to make a difference. Pray first for your own relationship with God, then you can hear the Spirit's direction as to how to pray for others. Intercessory prayer offers a golden opportunity to enlist in God's army of spiritual warriors. A prayer fellowship multiplies its effectiveness (Ecclesiastes 4:12). The church advances on its knees and is much in need of those who will give themselves to prayer. It's a hidden ministry on earth but certainly not in heaven. The hand of God is moved by the effective prayers of His people.

> - Do whatever good that comes to your hand day by day, and God will show you what the over-all pattern reveals for your life purpose. That's how Dr. Mark Buntain came to build a world famous hospital in Calcutta, India. (It was his mother's formula for finding and doing the will of God. He gave it to us as he spoke to the Bible School I attended in 1984.)

> - Submitting to one another establishes and holds the family of God together. Each person has a need for intimacy with significant others. As a single, you can fill that need by concentrating on loving relationships with friends. This does not include sexual intimacy, which must be met only within marriage.

As you guard your thought life and stay away from worldly stimulation, you can stay true to the purity the Lord asks of you and still be satisfied with your lot in life. Find intimacy on a level of mutual enjoyment, interests you share, building trust and caring about the concern of others. Be friends. And don't allow church-family squabbles to interfere in your relationship with God or people.

As a single adult, you live in relationship to others on a temporary basis. Therefore, the spiritual family you find in the fellowship of believers becomes an alternative to the identity and stability of a natural family. It also provides accountability, and reminds you that someone is watching your life.

Accountability And Submission

Accountability, through counsel and correction from time to time, is a safeguard that is needed by every Christian in some form if we are to stay on course. If you're allowing yourself to be held accountable to someone, you are, to that degree, in submission to them.

This was perfectly clear to the Puritans early in our country's history.

Christian Community as Family

While reading *The Light And The Glory* by Peter Marshall and David Manuel, I was impressed by a practice of the Puritans in the early days as they laid the spiritual foundations of our nation. The Puritans believed in the importance of families committed to each other in community living. Out of concern, they made it

123

a legal requirement that stable two-parent families take in single adults who could not afford a home alone. The single adult lived with the family as one of the children, in submission to its head.

The Puritans felt strongly the importance of a caring, concerned fellowship of the larger community for each of its people in order to promote the spiritual health, physical and social well being of the whole. They believed that to belong to Christ was to belong to each other. They lived the idealistic message found in the song, "The Family Of God," *When one has a heartache we all shed a tear.*[1]

Conquering the Mountain

Is fear of rejection a mountain for you? Do you feel it's hopeless for you to expect to fit into the Christian family? Don't let fear of rejection rob you of being a blessing and obeying God. Fear has to vacate the premises when trust in God and His love moves in. "There is no fear in love. But perfect love drives out fear, . . ." (1 John 4:18).

Be encouraged, keep a positive attitude, and smile a lot. A winning smile will do wonders toward building bridges for friendships. With friendships will come a sense of worth, which will give you victory over rejection. Make life fun if you can—a good sense of humor will open doors for you and brighten the day for those around you.

True, the church should already be reaching out to its single people in acceptance and loving fellowship, but since that may not be the situation in which you find yourself, it's neither helpful nor right to take a 'woe is me' attitude and sit alone waiting for others to come to you, or to judge them because they don't.

The best approach to the problem is, as St. Francis said, to "light a candle rather than curse the darkness." We live in a world full of needs and God will direct you to the very place where you are needed most, and for which you are best suited.

Find a Need and Fill It

A principle that works well when you're learning to handle your own emotional pain is to find someone else who is in need and give of yourself to fill that need. Be a blessing to others for whom Christ died and, in so doing, a blessing comes your way in return. Jesus said, "It is more blessed to give than to receive" (Acts 20:35).

The servant life of Jesus is an example to every Christian, but especially to the single person. He was a single who gave His life as God's servant from the manger to the cross. During the three and one-half years of His ministry and in His substitutionary death He showed God's heart of love for a world gone wrong.

While in His earthly body, He lived the life that the church, as His corporate body, is to continue to live until He returns. He didn't promise it would be easy, but he did promise to be with us and to give us the power to succeed. There is real joy in serving others in Jesus' name. He said that even a cup of cold water given in His name would not go unrewarded (Mark 9:41).

When people see Jesus' love expressed through one of His own, it becomes reality to them. His love restores the hope that many have lost, and without hope this world is indeed a dark place.

The only way those who need help can experience the love of Jesus is for His people to go to them in His name, ministering to the needs of those who will receive Him. If we have eyes with which to see and ears with which to hear, there are opportunities all around us.

The real need in the world is to be found beyond the church walls among those people who would not come or feel welcome at a church service. To go out where they are and bring the Kingdom of God to them is to follow the Lord's example. This is the kind of ministry to which a group of single people without family demands are often well suited.

Serving Within The Church

There are many possibilities for service within the activities of the church. I have seldom known a church that had enough dedicated people in children's ministries. To be involved in the life of a child is a special privilege for one willing to invest in the kingdom of God through touching a child's heart—it's the next best thing to parenting.

Another suggestion. If the desire of your heart is to serve where the need is greatest without regard to the status of the work, there is always a need for office chores and maintenance duties. As the old saying goes, it's amazing how much good you can do if you don't care who gets the credit.

Serving as unto the Lord requires expecting the rewards to come from Him rather than people. It also requires being able to submit to His Lordship over your activities, attitudes and relationships.

God's Approval Determines True Worth

Beware of sinful submission. It's especially important for singles to be selective in that to which they submit, and that they be able to discern and recognize when being a man-pleaser is robbing them of a closer relationship with God.

Allowing life to be lived according to the pleasure and approval of others is not the same as living the life of a servant that pleases God. When the eye is on performing in order to receive the approval of people, you're headed for shipwreck at some point down the road.

God sees the motivation of the heart, and His value of you is based on your relationship to His Son through His cleansing blood—not on what you do.

Desiring the approval of God—for who you are, not what you do—should blind you to the approval or disapproval of others. Your true worth comes only from His approval. Hopefully there will be those whose hearts are with you, and for that you will be thankful. But you will be deaf to praise and blame alike when your focus is on pleasing and obeying your heavenly Father rather than men.

The Single Parent

If life has handed you the challenge of single parenthood, there is an added dimension to deal with. You have double responsibilities, usually accompanied by diminished resources. Single parenting is one of life's most difficult assignments, and occurs all too often. It's the one that seems to be the least recognized and appreciated by the church fellowship. God, however, is not unaware of the difficulties you are going through, and He cares about you and will help you.

When you've experienced the devastation of losing a mate, either by divorce or death, life gets more than difficult. You feel that half of you is missing. And if the attitude of your church fellowship changes so that you no longer fit into your familiar place, you feel as if the rug has been pulled out from under you. It's a painful discovery and experience if it happens. Even though others who share the problems of a single life are best equipped to understand what you're going through, you need more than understanding—you need church people to be family.

If needed, perhaps there's something you can do to bring awareness to your church of the opportunity to help others in similar circumstances. Often that's what is needed to begin a ministry that wins people to the Lord. That would be a good alternative to harboring negative feelings about why somebody isn't doing something.

We tend to expect church leaders to be more than they can be. The closer a family is the more aware we are of the imperfections of its members and the more need there is for loving and forgiving each other. The same holds true for a church family. Keep this in mind as you form the bonds that go with commitment. If you do, you'll become a part of the solution and not part of the problem.

Ministering to Children

As I mentioned before, one of the most rewarding and needed jobs in the church is in children's ministry. Working with children is an investment in the future. It presents a challenge and an opportunity, because God has been stripped from secular education and entertainment. Church Bible classes are the only remaining support system for the Christian home. There you can be the teacher or activity leader that will be long remembered by the children for the influence of God in their lives. Children of all ages will respond to genuine love coming their way in the form of affection, food and fun in addition to teaching.

When you find a troubled child, he will need a trustworthy adult friend to turn to. As a single you can be that friend in whom he finds acceptance and from whom he will receive guidance. A Sunday School class provides an excellent opportunity for building relationships.

Be a good listener and a good friend in whom confidences can be shared. Trust has to be earned and must be treasured as you supply loving direction while instilling trust in God's grace and love for all His children.

These are just some of the possibilities for single people to serve the Lord. If you prayerfully look, you'll find many others that fit your situation.

As with all Christians, single people need to submit to God and to each other with specific accountability. The Body of Christ, in its healthiest form, is a spiritual family more real than a natural family. As such, submission and accountability, when properly addressed, finds its purest form of expression in the church fellowship.

As the Day of the Lord approaches, the Holy Spirit will, if we allow Him, bring us to a place of unity so that there is no lack of the practical contacts that make for healthy relationships in families as well as in the church.

Single people have many examples from the Scripture of those singles who were the movers and shakers in New Testament times. To a great extent, they were the ones God used to bring in the pure stream of God's grace and form the Church that turned the world upside down. As this age comes to a close, God will bring us full circle to the same flow of power the Church experienced in its beginning, perhaps using single people again in the same way.

As Jesus gets us ready to be taken out when He comes, there is much to be done. It will be a quick work, so prepare to be used by the Holy Spirit. Now, as in the beginning, single people are best equipped to be the catalyst for change because you, like the Apostle Paul, are free to devote yourselves to the work of God. If you're single, you have an open spiritual door before you. Go for it!

---

[1] "The Family of God" by William J Gaither, (© Copyrighted 1970 by William J Gaither. Published in *Hymns for the Family of God*, © Copyrighted 1976, Paragon Associates, Inc., Nashville, TN).

11

Slaves and Masters

Be A Living Witness

As you embrace the concept of living in submission to the will of God, your first thoughts should be how to apply it in the family and in church relationships. However, you will realize that it must also apply in the workplace if your Christian witness is to ring true. In the language of the Scriptures, the positions in the workplace are that of slaves and masters.

Usually the place you work is where you're in continual contact with the unsaved—the place, as the old saying goes, where the rubber meets the road. The reality of your Christian testimony is usually put to the test more in the workplace than anywhere else. Often there is not another Christian for your co-workers to observe, therefore it becomes doubly important that you represent Christ truly so they will be drawn to Him.

In that situation, you're an ambassador for Christ (2 Corinthians 5:20) right where you are. Jesus said, "let your light shine before men, that they may see your good deeds and praise your Father in heaven" (Matthew 5:16). In a dark place the light of a single candle shines brightly and can give light and hope to many. So, let your light shine where you are—and God will use it.

The most powerful spiritual tool you have is prayer for those with whom you work. But you will negate any good your prayers will do if you don't live before them in a manner that brings honor to the name of Jesus Christ.

The genuineness of your position in Christ will be tested every day in a variety of ways, so it will often be difficult just to hold your own without compromise. But never use that as an excuse to hide the fact that you're a Christian—doing so is only a form of denying Christ. God never promised an easy road, but He did promise to walk it with us (Isaiah 41:10).

Live What You Profess

Respect is an integral part of successful working relationships, and it goes both ways. With a life of integrity you give as well as earn respect. Your commission is, in the words of Jesus, "I am sending you out like sheep among wolves. Therefore be as shrewd as snakes and as innocent as doves" (Matthew 10:14).

God promises to give wisdom to those who ask for it (James 1:5), so ask Him for it and believe that He gives it to you. When His wisdom is applied it will help you to earn the respect of your co-workers. The Apostle James described godly wisdom for us: "But the wisdom that comes from heaven is first of all pure; then peace-loving, considerate, submissive, full of mercy and good fruit, impartial and sincere" (James 3:17). Also study the Book of Proverbs; it's God's storehouse of wisdom.

When you live a true Christian life before others, showing God's love and care for them, you may or may not see souls saved, but you're planting seeds that God will bring to harvest in His own time. Wherever you are, as a Christian you have it in your power to make things run smoother. Your presence on the job makes an avenue of blessing available to the whole place—and everyone in it.

The Importance of Attitude

Bringing a Godly attitude to work with you requires a willingness to be concerned about and submitted to the needs of others, no matter their status. This isn't to suggest that a Christian be a "submissive doormat"—that would create resentment and diminish respect. What we need to do is see others through the eyes of God's love and reach out to touch with His servant heart wherever we can. An attitude that values people makes the difference.

Jesus said, "The greatest among you will be your servant" (Matthew 23:11). To this end, the Apostle Paul said about himself, "I have become all things to all men so that by all possible means I might save some" (1 Corinthians 9:22).

Being thankful for the blessing of work brings the ability to cope with much in the way of irritations. There is great peace in giving thanks to God for the many blessings we tend to take for granted, and for the many things that in His sovereignty He brings into our lives. "Do not be anxious about anything, but in everything, by prayer and petition, with thanksgiving, present your requests to God" (Philippians 4:6, NIV).

And here's another great word from the Scriptures to help us find peace in everything. "Get rid of all bitterness, rage and anger, brawling and slander, along with every form of malice. Be kind and compassionate to one another, forgiving each other, just as in Christ God forgave you" (Ephesians 4:31-32).

Effectiveness of Prayer

In my early employment, I worked in an office with eight other ladies and one man, with another man as office manager. It was during the build-up of the war effort early in World War II so there was ample opportunity for advancement.

Because I was fresh out of school and anxious to do a good job, I moved up rather rapidly in position and pay. This caused jealousy among the others, and one older lady in particular. She had worked in this office for twenty years and I caught up with her position in two years without realizing I was in competition with anyone.

I had moved through most of the stations in the office until there was only one left for me to learn to be acquainted with all the operations. Then I was given an assignment that required I move into that last station. When the girl who held it flatly refused to teach me the routine, the boss said he would teach it to me. When her power play didn't work her jealousy surfaced in resentment and rejection.

It was during this time that I received Christ and was born again, and the resulting change in me seemed to aggravate the friction. The way things had gone from bad to worse was very troubling to me. I was in my early twenties and supporting myself, so leaving the job was not an option.

I didn't feel I had done anything wrong, but I also knew I had a responsibility as a witness to Christ's love to do what I could to make it right. I was certain that for me to be the cause of disharmony was not a good testimony to the others. Then one day as I was reading my Bible, the Lord impressed me with Matthew 5:44: "Love your enemies, bless them that curse you, do good to them that hate you, . . ." (KJV).

This was a command from my Lord that challenged everything in me. I went down the list of His orders and checked my inner spirit as I read each one. In searching my heart, I found I wasn't capable of genuine love for her at that time. A blessing would have been hollow and doing good would have seemed hypocritical. It troubled me that in all honesty I didn't have it in me to do those things—until I came to the last part of that verse, "and pray for them which despitefully use you and persecute you; That ye may be the children of your Father which is in heaven."

In that part of the verse I saw a command I could *willingly* obey. I said, "Yes, Lord, I can truly pray for her." The love of Jesus gave me a submissive attitude so that in prayer I could see her from the perspective of God's compassionate heart.

When I began to pray for her and all the difficulties I knew to be in *her* life, an amazing transformation began to take place in *me*. I no longer saw her through the eyes of the problems she was causing me, but through the eyes of God's love and concern for her. As a consequence, the animosity faded away—and so did the frustration. Although I didn't see a lot of change in her and we never became good friends, there was such a dramatic change in my attitude toward her that it relieved the tension of the whole office. Rather than adversaries, I found I had associates, people with whom I could work. With the conflict submitted to the Lord, the rest of my time in that office was easier and far more pleasant.

Because of the lessons I learned from that experience, I have many times recommended dealing with an enemy through forgiveness and prayer. You cannot continue to hate someone when you are sincerely praying God's love and blessing on them at the same time.

If you're willing to let go of the animosity—or at least willing to be made willing, God will replace it with His love and compassion. When He does, you'll find that behind the other person's ill will toward you is usually a hurting heart who needs the comfort and healing love of Jesus.

To Submit Willingly to Superiors—Know Who You Are

Do you have a problem submitting to your "superior"? Remember that person is superior only because of the job they hold, not because of a greater personal value. Their job may actually be of less practical value. Often it's the case that you could function without their being there, but their job would be meaningless without what you're doing.

God's view of the value of each individual is equal, be he a peasant or a king. When your sense of self-worth is defined by God, and is intact, it's not demeaning to you to willingly submit to the authority over you. The Christ-pleasing attitude is found in Paul's letter to the Ephesians: "Slaves [employees], obey your earthly masters with respect and fear, and with sincerity of heart, just as you would obey Christ. Obey them not only to win favor when their eye is on you, but like slaves of Christ, doing the will of God from your heart" (Ephesians 6:5-6).

Instructions for the boss is in another verse as Paul speaks to masters: "And masters, treat your slaves [employees] in the same way. Do not threaten them, since you know that he who is both their Master and yours is in heaven, and there is no favoritism with him" (Ephesians 6:9).

Paul's epistle to Philemon sheds more light on this subject . The Apostle is writing to him as a convert to Christ. Philemon was a slave owner and Paul writes concerning a runaway slave by the name of Onesimus. Slavery was a common practice in those days and was to them a form of employment.

Evidently Onesimus had been a rascal, and in his escape and wanderings had encountered the aged Paul who won him to Christ and had made him a well-established disciple. Paul pleads with Philemon to receive him as a brother in the Lord, an equal who will serve him well.

We see in this story an example of Paul's teaching concerning a right relationship between a boss (slave owner) and a worker (the slave) who was willing to submit to his "superior" of his own free will.

Submission, remember, is something you give. The work place is an important part of your life and is often the testing and proving ground of your Christianity. It takes commitment, training, perseverance, vision, and God's grace to overcome your natural tendencies under the adverse conditions you sometimes have to work. But, with God's help, all things are possible.

Significance of Work For a Man

God is interested in the family. He has prepared women to be best suited for primary care of the home and the nurture of its children. He has given to man the attributes of physical strength along with mental and emotional qualities that best equip him to be the provider and protector. God said, "By the sweat of your brow you will eat your food until you return to the ground" (Genesis 3:19a, NIV). That means a man must work throughout his life to provide for his family and himself.

A man is emotionally best equipped to take the wider view of the family's needs beyond hearth and home. The phrase, "couldn't see the forest for the trees," may apply to the way a woman views her world, but a man tends to see the forest and be less aware of the trees.

Each one needs the other's point of view so that together they can see life in a fuller dimension. Men and women are essentially different for a purpose, and to try to put them in the same mold flies in the face of reality for either one.

Men can and do take care of a home, and women can and do hold responsible jobs, but today's attitude of equality adds stress to the family and weakens its future. This position also does a disservice to women who, upon being awakened later in life to their nesting instincts, discover the value and rewards of bearing children. Then they learn it's too late.

A man, on the other hand, never out-distances his need for fulfilling his role as provider and ability to have children. Because of his very nature, a vocation is an important source of significance and meaning for a man's life. The essence of manhood from creation is to be a father, the definition of which is source, provider and protector for the family.

As father of the human race, Adam was given work to do by God. Just as in the pattern laid down for the first man, every man still needs a job. It gives him a sense of satisfaction about his accomplishments. When this is not there, a void is created in his sense of purpose.

Some work at jobs in which they take little satisfaction, but remain faithful to it because of the need for an income. In that case they develop hobbies that give them a significant substitute for identity with a distasteful job. The substitute satisfies the need for accomplishment, without which no man is complete.

Compare unemployment to being cut away from shore and cast adrift on the ocean without an anchor. The obvious need is for income and making a living, but the deeper need for significance remains when the need for income is no longer there. Men who have retired with an adequate income must fill this need, or their psychological and physical health will suffer. Even men who are wealthy have to find something to give life meaning other than self indulgence if they're to have a good quality of life.

Former President Carter continues his very worthwhile contribution to society by building houses for the needy through "Habitat For Humanity." And the purpose of the Ford and Rockefeller foundations was to use some of their great wealth to establish philanthropic institutions. Managing these enterprises became a job for them—and for their sons after them.

Looking to a Long-Range Goal

The reason for employment is deeper than a paycheck, vital though it is. Employment with a long-range goal gives purpose and meaning other than existing from one day to the next. Often seeing the goal is simply a matter of attitude. A vision for something greater than yourself gives dignity to the most menial of tasks.

If he sees it as such, the brick layer is building a beautiful house that will shelter a family. The mechanic is providing safe travel for people who will use a plane or drive the car. If you're in the military, your service is keeping our country and its people safe from potential enemies.

As your wages buy life's necessities, the security and confidence of your family brings great satisfaction. Their emotional stability is established as day follows day into the future, and so your goal is to build a future for your family.

These are temporal things, to be sure, but God recognizes earthly needs and provides for their fulfillment. This life is a testing ground to prepare us for eternity. The way we learn to obey and follow Him here and now makes a difference in forever—not for us only but for all those whom our lives touch.

The way of the Cross is the way of sacrificial commitment to duty, even if it's in the everyday humdrum of responsibility on a not too satisfying job. As you keep your long-range goal in mind, the immediate irritations that you encounter through the day lose their importance and power over you.

Holding to Righteousness

Let's go back to the basic principles of submission under God. If you are asked to do something illegal or against your standards as a Christian, your submission to God determines your conduct. Have the faith and courage to reject unrighteousness. On the other hand, if it's only your pride that's at risk, remember what Lucifer's pride cost him and be willing to let it go.

If you're persecuted because of your godly principles, remember what Jesus said: "But I say unto you, Love your enemies, bless them that curse you, do good to them that hate you, and pray for them which despitefully use you, and persecute you; That you may be the children of your Father which is in heaven: for he maketh his sun to rise on the evil and on the good, and sendeth rain on the just and on the unjust" (Matthew 5:44-45, KJV).

God's Word through the Holy Spirit will guide you in resolving conflicts, on the job as well as elsewhere. The name of Jesus Christ will be honored and you will become an effective witness for Him to your co-workers.

Other Scriptures on Work Relationships

> Slaves, submit yourselves to your masters with all respect, not only to those who are good and considerate, but also to those who are harsh. For it is commendable if a man bears up under the pain of unjust suffering because he is conscious of God. But how is it to your credit if you receive a beating for doing wrong and endure it? But if you suffer for doing good and you endure it, this is commendable before God. To this you were called, because Christ suffered for you, leaving you an example, that you should follow in His steps.   (1 Peter 2:18-21)

> However, if you suffer as a Christian, do not be ashamed but praise God that you bear that name. For it is time for judgment to begin with the family of God; and if it begins with us, what will the outcome be for those who do not obey the gospel of God?
>   (1 Peter 4:16-17)

For even when we were with you, we gave you this rule: "If a man will not work, he shall not eat." We hear that some among you are idle. They are not busy; they are busybodies. Such people we command and urge in the Lord Jesus Christ to settle down and earn the bread they eat. And as for you, brothers, never tire of doing what is right.

(2 Thessalonians 3:10-13)

12

The Christian and Government

Established by God

God originated government and its function. The Scriptures tell us God holds us accountable for respect and obedience to authorities (Romans 13:1-7). We dare not assume that we're above the law of the land because we're Christians. When there is a conflict between government and God's law, however, we must obey God (Acts 4:19, 5:29). Sorting out the mix is what this chapter is about.

The Apostle Paul wrote to the Roman Christians:

> Everyone must submit himself to the governing authorities, for there is no authority except that which God has established. The authorities that exist have been established by God.
>
> Consequently, he who rebels against the authority is rebelling against what God has instituted, and those who do so will bring judgment on themselves.

> For rulers hold no terror for those who do right,
> but for those who do wrong. Do you want to be free
> from fear of the one in authority? Then do what is
> right and he will commend you.   (Romans 13:1-3)

The assumption Paul makes is that government is basically upholding order and right. What, then, do you do when there is terror for doing right?

Persecution of Christians around the world indicates that the issue needs to be made clear. What is to be our position when and if our government becomes the adversary to the Christian life, as seems to be in the offing?

The problem is deep seated, having been progressively entrenched during the last seventy plus years. In the minds of many informed people, the crisis alarm is sounding now. There is an army of concerned citizens, mostly Christians, who are devoting their lives and careers to moving the hand of God to intervene for the return of righteousness. Those willing to expose themselves to the political and cultural battle are the brave soldiers of this generation.

As we exercise our God-given responsibility with regard to government, we need to know who those soldiers are. We are told to pray for them and for all who are in authority. As decisions are being made that will affect our children's future and our freedom to worship, we need to know who and what to support in government positions. To do so, we need to stay alert and informed.

There are Godly men and women holding political office and spearheading the return to righteousness. They need to know they have our support.

Put legs to your prayers and let your voice be heard, both at the voting booth and by contacting your representatives in government. They do listen. If the tide does not turn again toward righteousness, our freedom to worship God may soon be gone.

Identifying the Dangers

Through changes in religion, education, politics and finances, we have witnessed the undermining of the godly principles upon which this country was founded. The changes have been brought about on all fronts by those who advocate the liberal agenda and by the news media that supports them.

Many of its promoters are sincerely well-intentioned, though sincerely wrong from God's perspective. Those doing the promoting are easy to spot by the common beliefs and values they espouse: evolution, humanism, socialistic thought, and sympathy for any cause that promotes self-indulgence and immorality. In recent times, Christian bashing has become a popular liberal sport. The spirit of Anti-Christ is alive and well in America.

The Four Challenges
1. Religion

> It's time for the Church to wake from her slumber and act like the spiritual army she's called to be. The call is to "put on the whole armor of God, that ye may be able to stand" against the encroachment of the enemy (Ephesians 6:11). The purpose of the armor is to enable you to stand.

When the Church stands, Jesus promised that "the gates of Hades will not overcome it" (Matthew 16:18). The army will advance behind the Holy Spirit's use of the sword, which is the Word of God.

The enemy is obviously not expecting that to happen as his emissaries get bolder and bolder. Satan thinks he has the Church on the run but God has a plan. It is the Church militant, empowered by the Holy Spirit.

The religious challenge is primary because, behind the scenes, the battle is spiritual. One of the enemy's big guns has been thirty plus years of the Supreme Court's liberal interpretation of the Constitution. What Congress is forbidden to do, the Supreme Court has done by decision, repeatedly denying the right of Christian expression. This leaves no means of appeal for Christian citizens, except further challenges before the Court.

The First Amendment does not say, "separation of church and state." Rather it protects religious freedom against any restrictive laws Congress might make.

To quote from the Constitution, Amendment 1: "Congress shall make no law respecting an establishment of religion, or prohibiting the free exercise thereof." Clearly then, so long as the original intent of our Constitution is honored, we have law on our side.

President Ronald Reagan said, "The United States should never command worship or establish a state religion, but we poison our society when we remove its theological underpinnings. ... The truth is, politics and morality are inseparable and morality's foundation is religion. Religion and politics are necessarily related."[1] Time will prove him right.

Amid the gathering gloom, there is ample reason for hope. Godly legal organizations have been raised up to defend truth for Christians. Two of them making an impact are the American Center for Law and Justice and the Rutherford Institute.

Those in opposition to what Christians stand for are deceived by the promise of socialist thinking, which is the philosophy of liberals. They know that as long as the Christian underpinnings of this nation stay in place, socialism in any form cannot survive.

Loyalty to God, and loyalty to the state—which liberals idealistically espouse—are as light and darkness. Their ideology fits perfectly with the prophecies of a one world government under the antichrist. And so the followers of Christ, and anything related to Him, become a target.

How do we as Christians deal with it when push comes to shove? We need to be prepared to stay true to God, regardless of the consequences. To do otherwise is tantamount to following the enemy. One thing we must remember is to respect the authority, even though we must obey God's higher authority. There is no room for rebellion.

The early Church leaders handled it this way: "Peter and the other apostles replied: 'We must obey God rather than men'"! (Acts 5:29). By so saying, they risked punishment or even death, and were beaten and released. Knowing this was the will of God for them, they left the council, "rejoicing because they had been counted worthy of suffering disgrace for the Name" (Acts 5:41).

2. *Education.*

Education is the pivotal factor in shaping and molding a culture. The seed of socialism was planted a century ago in the top universities of England and America. Accordingly, determined to leave God's

redeeming work out of their agenda, liberal
educators, Church leaders and politicians
have for years been laying the foundation for
the present moral and spiritual decline.
Their success can be demonstrated by the
fact that we are no longer a true Christian
nation. In fact, our nation's cultural climate
has become anti-Christian.

The change in America's education profile began at the top level of learning and gradually filtered down through the system. Basic to its success has been the teaching of the theory of evolution as fact. Consequently, the effect of godlessness is now so deeply entrenched that most of our young people have nothing of substance on which to base their lives. The philosophy of humanism that is being offered is a poor substitute for faith in God.

History, as it is now being taught in our schools, is strangely silent on the godly foundation that gave America her strength. The theory of evolution is still being taught as an unequivocal fact despite increasing evidence to the contrary. Consequently, the young fall easy prey to the deception that camouflages the evils of the oncoming world ruler.

Having been robbed of knowledge of God, this generation of young adults are by and large without moral values, without hope, and without purpose. Because of the abortion issue, they also are without a sense of the value of life itself. As a result, they could be the generation that instigates persecution of Christians. The distortions and lies they have been fed will justify their actions in their own minds and hearts, as was the case in Hitler's Germany concerning the Jews.

On the other hand, many feel that out of this generation will come the energy and commitment for the next outpouring of the Spirit of God. When they are reached with the Gospel of Christ these people will know, better than others, the value of the light they have been given. When such a revival comes, it will be the job of established Christians to disciple the new converts and guide them on the right path. God will use us in the relationship chain to pass on the pure life of Christ to these coming soldiers of the Cross. Some Christians are even now being set aside by the Holy Spirit for training in the pure gospel. You will know if you're one of these.

In the meantime, know that Satan has the seduction of our young at the top of his list. Consequently, the education of our children must be watched closely to counteract any wrong influence coming from the system.

3. The Economy.

The economy began its downward slide with the Great Depression of the Thirties, followed in the Forties by the enormous expense of World War II. The concept of borrowing from future generations to enjoy current prosperity became an accepted mindset as economists planned an ongoing pattern of national debt.

It was under President Franklin Roosevelt's "New Deal" in the mid-thirties that, for the first time, federal government work programs provided much needed jobs at the expense of the taxpayer. The Social Security system came next, followed by the withholding of income taxes to make them less painful.

At that time also, we went off the gold standard and to the Federal Reserve system, thus making a way for our country's finances to be out of the control of the people and in the hands of a few powerful banking interests.

Step-by-step our once strong economy has been, in only seventy years, brought down so that now we face an incredible four-trillion-dollars-plus national debt. There is slim hope of ever pulling out of it. Revelation 13:16-17 reveals the economic plans the antichrist has in store for the world under his one world system:

> He also forced everyone, small and great, rich and poor, free and slave, to receive a mark on his right hand or on his forehead,
>
> so that no one could buy or sell unless he had the mark, which is the name of the beast or the number of his name.

But a strong national economy could successfully resist this.

The mark of the beast has been discussed for years. Now it's possible. For the first time in history, there is technology to implement it world wide. It seems that we're falling right into his plans. When that money system is implemented throughout the world perhaps it will also be the wake-up call for the Church. We dare not be caught napping.

What can we do to offset it? Study Revelation chapter thirteen to see what the challenges will be. If the return of the Lord does not deliver us out of this part of the great tribulation, be prepared to manage without money, and to die rather than take the mark. Knowing God and trusting in Him for everything we need is the only thing that will see us through until He takes us home. The timing of the rapture of the Church is debatable. The difficulties during the great tribulation are not.

4. *Politics.*

> Beginning in the thirties, appeal to the masses at the voting booth through government handouts allowed power to be vested in the hands of the instigators of these problems. Politicians found the proverbial goose that laid the golden egg.

Perpetuating the pattern of the Roosevelt era, liberal politicians continue to promise that government will take care of people in need. A self-indulgent society tends to think only of "What can I get?" not "Where is it coming from?" or "Where are we going?" The net effect is that votes are bought and paid for with our tax money.

Our weapon against this encroachment on our way of life is that we all exercise our responsibility to vote. Resist the mindset of dependency on government wherever you can. Learn what is going on so that you vote wisely, but vote. And pray. Get involved.

I've given a historical thumbnail sketch of the four problems that caused our present mess. Hopefully it will help you understand how we got here, and where hope lies. Do what you can to influence change where it is needed, then pray for God's guidance and protection through whatever lies ahead. The early Church faced difficult times before us. Let us learn from them.

Difficulties in New Testament Times

Throughout the writing of the New Testament, God's people were under persecution. They were still close to the social dynamics that sent Jesus to the Cross, but also to the eyewitness testimonies of the awesome power that resurrected Him. Because it was pertinent to their lives, there are many statements in the epistles on how Christians should response to persecution.

They were never instructed to go on the offensive against their persecutors, nor were they told to submit to their demands. They were to go undaunted about the business of obedience to God, and suffer the consequences of refusing to obey ungodly demands in the same spirit of power and love with which Jesus went to the cross. Submission to government orders was simply superseded by submission to Ultimate Authority: God.

When Peter and John were given orders to speak no more in the name of Jesus following a miraculous healing, they answered, "Judge for yourselves whether it is right in God's sight to obey you rather than God. For we cannot help speaking about what we have seen and heard" (Acts 4:19-20).

For a Christian, confrontation with the powers of this world is inevitable. Jesus said, "If the world hates you, keep in mind that it hated me first." (John 15:18).

And the Apostle Paul said, "everyone who wants to live a godly life in Christ Jesus will be persecuted, while evil men and impostors will go from bad to worse, deceiving and being deceived" (2 Timothy 3:12-13).

Not only do the Scriptures tell us we will be persecuted, Jesus told us how to respond to our persecutors: "Love your enemies, bless them that curse you, do good to them that hate you, and pray for them which despitefully use you, and persecute you" (Matthew 5:44, KJV).

Our Lord also told us what our attitude is to be during persecutions: "Rejoice and be glad, because great is your reward in heaven, for in the same way they persecuted the prophets who were before you" (Matthew 5:12). Notice that He did not say to rejoice and be exceedingly glad because of the persecution but because of the reward we would receive in heaven. Look at Acts 5:41 again. The apostles rejoiced that they had been counted worthy to suffer for His name.

When the time of persecution arrives for us, the presence of the Holy Spirit will strengthen us so that we'll be able to stand firm and obey God, as He has strengthened and enabled our brothers and sisters in Christ throughout the history of the Church.

Old Testament Examples

Some of the most encouraging stories of the Old Testament tell of heroes of the faith who stood tall against a government determined to destroy their witness for God. Let's look at three of them: Moses; Shadrach, Meshach, and Abednego; and Daniel.

Moses

Moses' birth is a biblical example of putting faithfulness to God ahead of obedience to governmental authority. The midwives in Egypt were ordered by Pharaoh to kill all the Israelite boy babies in order to stop the population growth of the Jewish slaves (Exodus 2:1-15).

They opposed him and God honored their stand by bringing out of those babies the one who was to be their deliverer. Moses became the leader whom God used, not only to lead the nation across the Red Sea to freedom, but to give them leadership through the first forty years of their life as a nation.

It was to him that God gave the Ten Commandments and the Old Covenant laws, which form the foundation for law in Great Britain and the United States to this day.

Shadrach, Meshach and Abednego

In another example, we have the three Hebrews in the fiery furnace of Nebuchadnezzar's Babylon. They were ordered to bow down to the image that the king had made. The penalty for refusal was death.

Their reply was, "O Nebuchadnezzar, we do not need to defend ourselves before you in this matter. If we are thrown into the blazing furnace, the God we serve is able to save us from it, and He will rescue us from your hand, O king. But even if He does not, we want you to know, O king, that we will not serve your gods or worship the image of gold you have set up" (Daniel 3:16-18).

They did not know that God would deliver them but their loyalty belonged to Him regardless. The outcome of that defiance of the Emperor's orders was a miraculous deliverance that so impressed Nebuchadnezzar that it changed the course of history at the very beginning of the Gentile age, some 2,500 years ago.

Daniel

It was under another king, Darius, that Daniel, who in his youth had also been taken into Babylonian captivity, defied the orders of the king and continued to pray three times a day. His punishment was to be thrown into the den of lions to be torn in pieces by them.

But God had other plans. Through His faithful servant, Daniel, God showed His power to shut the mouths of hungry lions in honor of His beloved servant (Daniel 6:1-28). He later gave Daniel prophecy for the time of the end of the ages.

Just as He has done throughout the ages, God will still take care of His own who put their trust in Him.

Let us thank God for the government we still have, doing what we can to preserve its goodness. However, we must be on guard against allowing ourselves to be deceived into participating in its sins.

Whatever the future holds for the Church and the world around us, the end of the Bible tells us that we win. Jesus said, "When these things begin to take place, stand up and lift up your heads, because your redemption is drawing near" (Luke 21:28).

[1] "President Ronald Reagan," by John Johnson (© Copyrighted 8-24-84, *Sacramento Bee Newspaper*, Sacramento, CA.).

13

Emotional Hindrances to Submission

Why is it so difficult to submit to others, even when it's God's command? For that matter, why is it so difficult to surrender unconditionally to God's will, even when we know His will is best for us? What are the emotions that fill us up and block the pathway to the healing love of Jesus? And where do they come from?

Any experience in our past that has left scars of fear, bitterness, unforgiveness, anger, inability to trust, etc., can prevent us from growing emotionally and spiritually. A repeated pattern of sinful and self-justified reactions to offenses becomes the substance of strongholds that the enemy of our soul will use to defeat us and hold us captive.

Having been erected as a defense against further pain, they become a wall that keeps healing out. Strongholds are made of wrong thinking and wrong decisions that have formed wrong attitudes and habits. It's through these strongholds that we give the devil access to attack our spirit and deceive us.

Sadly, even the pre-born and infants can establish strongholds unless someone stands in prayerful guard over their spirits. Don't get me wrong. I'm not saying that an infant is held accountable for the sin. I am saying that, even though a baby is innocent of personal guilt, he will, in his spirit, react to his pain according to mankind's fallen state.

Without the prayer covering of a caring adult, he's incapable of a godly response to negative stimuli. He then bears the impact of wounding within himself. Parents may or may not be able to guide him through the fallout from it. Since he senses a lack of protection, fear, which is at the root of other negative emotions, then gets a foothold. As he matures and problems present themselves, the solution is to teach him to face them with a forgiving heart. Because of a wounded spirit, however, he may be incapable of doing so. We will come back to this.

The younger the person, the more impact any experience leaves. Therefore, when an adult is psychologically wounded, the scars are not as deep as those in a child and they are more easily identified. It can still be a devastating experience, but he has more of life behind him with which to handle the problem. A responsible adult can choose to accept the challenge of obedience to God's rules of problem relationships, which are confrontation and forgiveness.

When we struggle, however, with the submission God commands we expose a need to understand God's wisdom in it. We deal with the immediate circumstances but He sees from an eternal perspective. Failing to recognize His protection and plan will foster an unloving attitude, thus closing the door to a submissive spirit. It's these closed doors we will now examine.

Hurtful Experiences

Rejection is one of our most painful emotions and it can leave its victim feeling unloved, insecure, unworthy, and in fear of abandonment. When rejection is in the spirit from babyhood, parental discernment is needed in order to understand any ensuing problems the child may have.

Another hurt is abuse, both physical and emotional, which leaves its victims feeling guilt, shame, in fear of people, or seeking acceptance through unhealthy physical love. Whatever it is, the effect of those painful experiences, and the responses to them, form a veil through which future experiences are filtered. A person who is struggling with those memories will find submission inordinately difficult, because submission requires a trusting heart—the very thing that has been stolen.

Submission seems to demand that this person now let go of the protective shell he has erected. In doing so, he fears becoming vulnerable again to the kind of thing that caused his pain in the first place. He would be giving away whatever precious autonomy he's managed to hold on to. Knowing the security of God's unconditional love gives courage to take the risk. Without that security, the unregenerate heart must rely on natural understanding, based on self-interest and self-protection, while a person who has a relationship with God through Jesus Christ has Heaven's resources at his command.

Jesus was compelled by love when He submitted to His Father and left Heaven to enter into our need. As His followers, we have as our goal to be free of anything that would keep us from loving with that same abandon, so that we can enter into the needs of others in His name. That is, in essence, godly submission. To love one

159

another is His command. It follows then that we need to identify any hang-ups that get in the way of loving relationships.

The most likely place to find the source of problems is in both the natural family and in the family of God. It is in these relationships, with the most potential for help and healing, that unforgiveness most easily rears its ugly head.

The Healing Power of Forgiveness

When we refuse to forgive someone for any offense, no matter how damaging, we deny the message of Jesus and His work on the cross. He taught forgiveness throughout His three and one-half years of ministry, and it was on His lips as He breathed His last. He who had no need of being forgiven suffered more wrong than any man who ever lived; yet Jesus was the most ardent advocate of forgiveness. He then became its highest example.

In the light of this truth, how can we, who have received Christ's forgiveness through His death and resurrection refuse to forgive another for whom He also died? Especially when we're the ones most damaged by our refusal to forgive.

Here we see the real issue. Why not forgive? Usually the reasoning is something like: "The person inflicted so much pain on me! Life would have been okay otherwise. What happened was not my fault." Our sense of justice demands a penalty for a wrong act and so we hold tenaciously to the need to see it dealt with, or at least see a sign of the offending person's regret for what they did to us. That sense of justice is God-given, but with a twist. God holds the penalty for sin in His own hands. We take it upon ourselves at our peril.

The secret of successful forgiveness is to release judgment and any required punishment to God, He'll take care of it. As Paul wrote: "Do not take revenge, my friends, but leave room for God's wrath, for it is written: 'It is mine to avenge; I will repay,' says the Lord" (Romans 12:19).

Don't even try to hang on to any supposed right to see if or how God does it—simply know that He will, as only He knows how. Trust Him to do right and let it go. When you do, you'll be free to see the person who hurt you as one in need of God's redemptive love and you can pray for them. Jesus commanded us to pray for our enemies. Therefore, it's a key to our healing.

In dealing with our reluctance—and sometimes inability—to forgive, the beginning of the solution lies in facing the fact that what is done cannot be undone, no matter what we do or how much we wish it could. Time and events are not revocable. The fact is that another way must be found to acquire inner peace.

Many things will happen in our lives that will require us to forgive someone. Some experiences will be unspeakably difficult in anyone's language, while others will be relatively small and easy to forgive. Whatever the hurts, if we hold the offenses in our hearts we will suffer the damaging effects of unforgiveness.

Unforgiveness stops the flow of God's Holy Spirit into our lives and with it the blessings and joy He wants to give to us. Without forgiveness the offender is kept in our lives because the emotions and memory keep him there. If we want to be free, each time we remember the hurt we must let it go—releasing it to a holy, righteous, and loving God. Soon you will be free.

Dealing With Anger

Having dealt with the crippling effects of unforgiveness, let us move on to some of the emotional difficulties it holds, such as anger and fear. (Bitterness and resentment will be dealt with in the next chapter.)

If the pain of a suffered wrong stays with you, it may present itself in the form of anger with an explosive potential. This anger can be tapped into when you feel threatened or devalued, especially by a reminder of the source of your pain. It is like a volcano waiting to erupt.

In stressful situations, it may turn to rage. You do not find satisfaction in expressing the rage, however, because your anger cannot be directed at the true source of the pain. The problem then gets worse. The longer you hold onto it, the more damage it does. So be quick to deal with it.

Until it is resolved, there needs to be a safe venting, because anger, when it is turned inward, is a major source of depression. Safe venting would include vigorous exercise, playing loud music, screaming into a pillow, hitting a punching bag or the like—to release emotional energy. When repressed anger is vented in the wrong way, it may damage property or people, or be evidenced by one lashing out at some unsuspecting victim who may be without a clue as to the real source of the anger. The relationships that are damaged when this is the case are usually the most important relationships in your life, since these are those involving the people with whom you have come to feel safe.

Protecting Relationships

If they are to last, these relationships are the ones most in need of the protecting power of the fruit of the Holy

Spirit, especailly love, patience, and gentleness—but all are necessary (Galatians 5:22-23). They give a quality of life that brings satisfaction, no matter with whom you interact. As you walk in faith, hope, and love (1 Corinthians 13:13), the fruit of the Holy Spirit will guide you toward a life in submission to God. When the presence of the Holy Spirit is embraced in our lives, the fruit will appear as naturally as fruit grows on a tree.

Surrender to God

The change that comes about in the process of surrendering to God takes place in the soul, wherein lies the mind, will, and emotions. When the mind understands the issues and desires to be healed, when the will determines to act on what the mind knows, the emotions are then challenged to agree.

Emotions

At that point, the issue is drawn because it is the emotions that rule much of our lives. If the emotions can be held captive to the old nature, we are the loser. It is through the emotions that we give access to our personal spirit. Thus, it becomes a spiritual battle, and godly submission is at the heart of it.

Emotions are not in and of themselves right or wrong. They are natural, God-given responses to experiences. It is what we do about them and with them that determines whether or not there is sin on our part. We are not responsible for what others do to us, but we are responsible for our reaction(s) to it. When the will is lined up with the spirit to do what pleases God, the emotions can be won over.

163

Choices—The Battleground

Although the battle is often difficult, with God's help we *can* choose a godly emotional reaction to offenses and adverse situations. Our reaction choice determines whether we win or lose the spiritual battle. Often emotional and spiritual health as well as eternal consequences hang in the balance. The forces of darkness are tenacious but, thankfully, God is eternally merciful and long-suffering toward His children and ever stretches forth His hand through Christ to help us in the battle.

Satan's hold on our emotions did not develop overnight—and will not dissipate overnight. God is capable of performing an instant miracle of deliverance and healing, of course, but usually allows time in the healing process for change in us to take place, because without a change in thought and living habits the old patterns will invite the problems to return. There is also no way for us to mature spiritually and emotionally without the on-going process of making godly choices and holding to them.

Holding Fast

Because of the disintegration of family life and escalating moral collapse of our culture, godly choices are not always clear or easy—and holding to them in the face of changing situations and times is sometimes difficult. Today there are generations of people who suffer the effects of society's ills and are without a moral compass. God alone has the solution, and He applies it one person at a time as we make ourselves available to Him and submit to His will.

Without submission there is no way that God can help us because in not submitting we have chosen to go our own way. Our submission to God, in turn, is determined by our relationship to Jesus Christ as our Lord. When we choose Christ as truly Lord over our life, then we choose to live in emotional and spiritual health. His eternal love for us, and our developing love for Him, will win over any adverse situations that confront us.

The Power of Love

There is a sense of power that comes from knowing who you are and being confident in that knowledge. Every person, whether Christian or non-Christian, has a need for this sense of power. The Christian, however, has a distinct advantage in that God has promised to believers the spirit of power and of love. The Apostle Paul said, "God has not given us the spirit of fear; but of power, and of love, and of a sound mind (2 Timothy 1:7, KJV) It's no accident that power, love, and a sound mind go together.

Power without love is dangerous. Yet, in order to freely love, we need to know we are coming from a position of confidence or power, and we need sound thinking to use it wisely. God uses this combination of spiritual assets—power, love, and a sound mind—to combat the destructiveness of the spirit of fear.

He gave power first because, in order to love unconditionally, we need a sense of His power as well as His love. This is in stark contrast to the spirit of fear, which does not come from Him. God then gives us a sound mind with which to guide our life.

To submit to another person in love and self discipline has power to influence the other person's life. That's because love and truth inspire confidence and win people, hence the connection between power, love, and a sound mind.

165

You surrender from a position of weakness. You submit to another from a position of power. When you surrender to God or man, you are declaring your weakness. When you submit to God or man, you declare the power of love.

Fear vs. Love

We tend to think of love and hate as opposites but in God's economy it is fear that is the opposite of love. Fear takes hold of the negative aspect of our nature and holds us back from a trusting relationship with God and man. This is the fear that's the arch enemy of love. That's why the Bible says, "There is no fear in love. But perfect love drives out fear, because fear has to do with punishment. The one who fears is not made perfect in love" (1 John 4:18). Examining the dynamics of fear and love will help us to understand.

You see, both fear and love are directional. Love flows outward and gives to the object loved, while fear pulls inward like a magnet to protect the self from outward intrusion. One gives life; the other absorbs it.

Love

Jesus said of those who believe on Him, "as the Scripture has said, streams of living water will flow from within him" (John 7:38). This is the Lord's way saying that love flows outward as a river. The living waters that flow out of us come from the fountainhead of God's love. As His love flows out of us, it washes away the negative self-love in us and makes us willing to spend and be spent for others. Thus we are able to live in submission both vertically and horizontally, in the same way that the Cross points up to God and reaches its arms out to the world.

Fear

Fear is an emotional magnet that draws everything inward. It then puts up a wall of protection behind which self cowers, not daring to hope for the light. Fear's thrust is to protect the self nature, keeping it hidden from that which would cause its sinfulness to be painfully exposed to the light of God's holiness. Jesus said, "This is the verdict: Light has come into the world, but men loved darkness instead of light because their deeds were evil. Everyone who does evil hates the light, and will not come into the light for fear that his deeds will be exposed. But whoever lives by the truth comes into the light, so that it may be seen plainly that what he has done has been done through God" (John 3:19-21).

The works of darkness are such things as pride, self-righteousness, rebellion, and the works of the flesh listed in Galatians 5:19-21. In contrast, the light awakens us to humility, faith, and hope, which abide in love. It is easy to see in which atmosphere a submissive spirit would be comfortable.

Behind the reason people are drawn to the evil deeds of the flesh is fear's protective shell around the emotions. It needs to be broken down in order to expose the truth and resist Satan's deceptive appeal. Look deep enough and you'll find his signature of fear. The antidote is faith and trust. The story of Job will inspire both.

Job's Trial

Love and submission can only operate in an atmosphere of trust, free of Satan's wiles. It was Job's proven trust in God, built throughout his lifetime, that enabled his faith to endure when he couldn't understand the reason for his pain. He had spent his lifetime getting to know the nature of God through an obedient relationship with Him. Because of that he couldn't understand why he was suffering. Nevertheless, that earliest of Old Testament saints said, "Though he slay me, yet will I hope in him" (Job 13:15). Job knew his integrity was intact, and according to his understanding, he met God's requirements for blessing, not trouble. Thus, his dilemma.

At the end of his trial, Job discovered a whole new dimension of God that he could not see before he was tested. He thought he had God all figured out when, to his dismay, God did something unexpected, which Job was not prepared to deal with on blind faith alone. Sound familiar? Unexpected stretching is still used by God to move us along to maturity.

After his testing was complete, God rewarded Job's trust by giving him double the blessings that he had enjoyed before (Job 42:12-17). Job's experience should shed some light on the security there is in trusting God and submitting to His will.

Some Final Thoughts

If you've had a bad experience with submission or feel you've been betrayed, you're not alone. As you deal with the hurt and disillusion, however, a caution is in order. Don't continue to hold the hurt inside lest the hurt become bitterness. Confront the issue with a forgiving spirit and avoid its snare.

If you can't submit without bitterness, don't. Consider our Lord's example. Don't submit to unrighteousness but get your attitude right. The Bible says, "Do nothing out of selfish ambition or vain conceit, but in humility consider others better than yourselves" (Philippians 2:3).

Forgiveness is always in order, no matter the offense. Check how you stand emotionally and be ready for reconciliation if it's possible. There's a subtle deceit in trying to avoid confrontation, either with yourself or someone else.

Without early resolution, the hurt becomes anger. Then, if not, dealt with and forgiven, it settles in as bitterness that is more damaging than hurt or anger. Bitterness is a poison to the spirit. After fear, it's the most damaging to the spirit.

As I said before, if memory of an offense is a problem, every time you think about it, forgive again. Jesus said to forgive seventy times seven (Matthew 18:22). After that who keeps score? Along the way you'll be set free. Deal with forgiveness as a fact, not a feeling.

Emotions are the driving force in life. They effect how we think and how we make decisions. When emotions are unhealthy, life cannot be filled with the joy and peace God intends His children to have. At Calvary, Jesus paid the price not only for salvation but also for healing of the whole person—spirit, soul, and body. This healing makes room for the blessing of submissive relationships.

14

Submission Without Bitterness

Avoiding Bitterness

Bitterness gets into your spirit when hurts you do not deserve remain unforgiven and turn into anger. Resentment follows and then settles in as bitterness, and the heart becomes hardened. The downward spiral through hurt, anger, resentment and bitterness must be broken if there is to be wholeness and health.

The way anger is handled is key to success. The Scripture says, "In your anger do not sin": Do not let the sun go down while you are still angry" (Ephesians 4:26). Obviously, anger is not of itself a sin. It's an emotion, and emotions are not sin. It's what you do with them that can be sinful.

Anger must be validated as real in order to be used as God intended. Don't bury it. Before the day is over, decide what your responsibility is and what you should do about it, then move on to confrontation because you care. As you do, work toward forgiveness. Reconciliation hopefully follows, but that requires two people willing to work at it.

If there is unresolved hurt and anger toward the person in a relationship requiring submission, you are not free to submit in love. Anything that blocks a free flow of love also hinders submission of the heart. Going through the motions of submission without a loving spirit can only foster inner resentment that, in time, becomes bitterness to the spirit. What is in the spirit cannot be hidden for long.

Like the little boy who was reprimanded for not sitting down. When he finally gave in and sat down he said, "I may be sitting down on the outside, but I'm standing up on the inside!" Until the issue is resolved in forgiveness, submission becomes "standing up on the inside."

Nothing of substance can be built on that kind of relationship. Submission is often handled in this way, however, so submission itself appears to be the problem. Troubling issues need to be dealt with honestly before entering into a commitment of submission. Willing submission is the goal.

The writer of Hebrews admonishes us, "See to it that no one misses the grace of God and that no bitter root grows up to cause trouble and defile many" (Hebrews 12:15).

Dr. S. I. McMillen, MD., in his best selling book, *None of These Diseases*, likens the poison of a bitter spirit to acid. He says, "What a person eats is not as important as the bitter spirit, the hates, the feelings of guilt that eat him. . . . acids that destroy body, mind and soul."[1] Thus he describes the physical price we pay when we fail to respond to the grace that God gives us.

To be most effective, our forgiveness will be at the point where hurt puts on anger as a defense against pain. Rev. Paul Goulet writes, "If unresolved hurt and anger is not caught at this point, the condition deteriorates into hate, resentment, bitterness and other painful emotions which will dominate and distort our lives."[2]

If spiritual health is to be maintained, each hurt must be met with a forgiving, non-judgmental attitude, thereby releasing into God's hands any judgment of the people who have hurt you. The Apostle Paul wrote, "Do not take revenge, my friends, but leave room for God's wrath, for it is written: 'It is mine to avenge; I will repay,' says the Lord" (Romans 12:19b).

You can trust God to vindicate you, so rest assured you are safe in releasing judgment to Him. Close that door tight. Don't even keep the privilege of checking to see what kind of vengeance God is doing or when. Just know that it's taken care of in righteousness, and you are vindicated without being guilty of having a judgmental spirit. You will then be free to obey God's command to love.

This is the shield of faith in operation as part of the spiritual armor of Ephesians 6:16. The shield can be moved around as needed to quench the fire of the enemy's darts, which are intended to inflict pain. If the darts don't get by your shield, the pain will not be there to initiate the anger, and the cycle is broken before it gets started.

In contrast, when these negative emotions are allowed access, and have settled into your spirit, the root of bitterness begins to do its damage and scatters its poison as it grows.

Except for a miraculous healing of the memories by the Holy Spirit, the way out of this dilemma is to go back in memory to where the problem originated. Own it as a fact of your past, but do what you can to erase its emotional hold on you. Confess your unforgiveness and ask the Lord to forgive you. You will then have a clean slate with which to take the necessary steps of confrontation with forgiveness and be set free.

Control Does Not Produce Submission

Where submission is seen as an issue of absolutes requiring unquestioning obedience to an authority figure, the person who is to submit finds his autonomy threatened. If he yields to that requirement, there is the danger of bitterness creeping into the heart as he chafes under its demands.

Often the person in the position of control is struggling with a wrong concept of what his responsibility is, so in reality he, too, is a victim of wrong teaching.

Two kinds of relationships are particularly vulnerable to the problem of inappropriate control because both demand our deepest heart commitment. One is the role of a husband or wife, and the other is the church where a pastor, by common practice and training, is made a ruler. Beware of allowing bitterness to get a foothold even though you see problems.

To break free of control without rebelling is to exercise tough love as you properly confront, forgive, and move on without the shackles of a bitter spirit. It means to establish and maintain proper boundaries between you and those in authority over or under you. Learn to trust God in the other person.

Scriptural Lessons On Bitterness

What can we learn about bitterness from the Scriptures? There's a story in the book of Exodus about how the children of Israel were delivered from Egypt, crossed the Red Sea, and then traveled three days into the wilderness (Exodus 15:23-25). They were in need of water, and, when they found it, the water was bitter, so they named the place Marah, which means bitter. The water was poison to them. They could not drink it and began to murmur against Moses.

Moses cried to the Lord for help and the Lord showed him a tree—or piece of wood—which Moses threw into the water, and the water became sweet—good to drink. About this incident and place, the Scripture says, "There the LORD made a decree and a law for them, and there he tested them" (Exodus 15:25b).

It was clear by the Israelites' reaction to the problem of bitter water that God still had more to teach them about trusting His faithfulness to provide for them in spite of circumstances. By complaining instead of trusting God to take care of them, they showed they had not learned the lesson of the Red Sea crossing. They were not yet ready for the battle that they would be required to fight when they entered the Promised Land—or even ready to trust God enough to enter the Promised Land, which was proved later.

The way in which bitterness is dealt with is still a testing ground for the Christian. Water alludes to the spirit. The tree that purified the water is a fore-shadowing of the wooden Cross on which Jesus died for the sins of the world. Just as the tree healed the bitterness of the water, so the work of the Cross provides the cure for bitterness of the human spirit. To avail yourself of its spiritual and emotional healing power, you must accept the work of Jesus and His provision. His blood shed on Calvary is sufficient for all your needs.

175

Let's look at another Old Testament example of testing. According to Moses' law, bitter water was used to prove the guilt or innocence of a woman accused of adultery by her husband (Numbers 5:11-31). At Marah, the whole nation under the Abrahamic Covenant was at risk and tested; in the case of adultery, one person under the Old Covenant was at risk and tested—both by bitter waters.

New Covenant Testing

The testing for New Covenant saints is more subtle but just as revealing. Often hidden bitterness is revealed in an unhealthy attitude toward life, in a lack of ability to love, in overcompensating by doing 'good works,' by withdrawing into a shell and holding others at arm's length, by a lack of inner peace, or stunted spiritual growth. It can even be camouflaged by over-zealousness in church work and faithful attendance, or it can cause people to break off relationships, and stop attending church altogether.

Regardless of the way bitterness is handled, there is always a negative effect on relationships until it is exposed to the light and corrected. It behooves us to be quick to respond when the Holy Spirit puts His finger of conviction on a problem area of our lives, identifying the poison that must be purged. That's the way of the winner.

Forgiveness is the Cure

As has been said before, the cure for this poisoned condition in the spirit is forgiveness. If you cannot honestly muster the resources for forgiveness, then recall the reality of your own sins and how much God has forgiven you. This will help you to identify with the other person's sin against you, and enable you to find that place in your heart to forgive as you've been forgiven.

Whatever your sins may be, they might not seem bad in the light of current social values, but in the light of God's holiness they separate you from Him. Unforgiveness has no place in the life of the Lord's servant. Jesus gave His life to pay its penalty so that you, as well as the one who has offended you, may be brought into fellowship with the Father.

It's on this basis that you can forgive anything, because God's willingness to forgive is unlimited, as He demonstrated at the Cross. Christ suffered the ultimate in spiritual and emotional, as well as physical pain, yet He forgave His tormentors from the Cross. And He still offers forgiveness to all who will come to Him.

When you have done all you can to resolve the issue between you and another person, it's helpful to move on to other places and interests. If memory still brings pain, choose with each remembrance to forgive again and again until the Lord has purged it from your emotion as well as your spirit. In the meantime, find new surroundings with new experiences for a healthier basis on which to build new memories

Forgiveness does not mean acceptance or approval of a wrong done to you—and restored relationship may or may not be forthcoming. It does mean, however, that you no longer hold the perpetrator accountable to you for a wrong you suffered at his or her hands.

When you release the person to accountability before God, you are then free to see that person through God's eyes of compassionate love. You can even be a vessel of His redeeming love to that person if He so directs you. If not, your responsibility is finished. Early re-establishment of the relationship is not necessarily included in forgiveness. That takes rebuilding of trust, which is another matter. It completes the process, but needs to be earned over a period of time.

Jesus said, "But I tell you: Love your enemies and pray for those who persecute you" (Matthew 5:44b). When you determine in your heart to pray for someone who has mistreated you, a wonderful thing begins to happen. As the Holy Spirit works in your heart you'll find that it's not possible to earnestly pray God's good for any person and still hold animosity toward them. So pray for them and watch the bitterness go.

Sometimes being willing to forgive is the hard part. The anticipation of revenge tastes so sweet, but don't be fooled. Its reality has a hollow ring. God reserves that responsibility for Himself and He not only can but will do right, in the light of both now and in eternity.

When you're willing to let go of your right to demand accountability or revenge, God works the miracle of forgiveness in your heart. As you assume His attitude and begin to see that Christ died for the sin of the one who hurt you, your perspective changes and you see hope for your own healing. As you go, you'll be washed clean of the negative emotions that have caused your pain.

This doesn't necessarily happen the first time you pray, because it's a process requiring a change of attitude that you may have held for a long time. Be persistent in obedience to His command, however, and you'll be rewarded, not only by the answered prayer for the other person but by a new freedom in your own spirit, and new trust in God.

Thankfulness

It is especially helpful in the emotional healing process to praise the Lord with your voice and be thankful. Praise and thanksgiving directs your thoughts to God and allows you to reaffirm faith and trust in Him. We should always praise Him because of who He is, and we should always be thankful for His blessings, which are many and which can easily be found if you look for them, even in the direst of circumstances.

The old hymn, *Count Your Blessings*, says it well:

> When upon life's billows you are tempest-tossed,
> When you are discouraged, thinking all is lost,
> Count your many blessings, name them one by one,
> And it will surprise you what the Lord has done.[3]

Don't wait until you feel thankful. Just remember how much He has done for you; thank Him because it is right to do so and right feelings will follow. Don't accept defeat—you can't afford it.

Unforgiveness that has turned into bitterness hurts the unforgiving victim more than the offender. However, you also hold that person bound to you when you refuse to loose him in forgiveness.

Physical and mental illness are often caused by the inability to release another person in forgiveness for suffered wrongs. The body reacts to problems in the spirit. Consequently, lack of spiritual health spills over into problems with physical health.

If you can't submit without bitterness, don't fool yourself into thinking that you can or should pretend to. Be honest with yourself and with God. He's not fooled. You can, however, act on fact rather than feeling.

Submission compelled by love is the only kind that works. Actions express love more than feelings. Feelings follow actions—do the right thing and right feelings will follow.

The Apostle Paul referred to himself as a love-slave of Jesus Christ. Now that is true submission at its best. Jesus said, "If you love me, you will obey what I command." (John 14:15).

Love for Christ is expressed in submissive obedience to His commandments. Love for people, which He commands, is expressed in submission to doing what you can to meet the true need of your neighbor. Love for God and people in a relationship of mutual submission is the key to providing the unity of spirit through which God's power can flow in our families and in our churches.

The Scripture says that Jesus is coming for "a radiant church, without stain or wrinkle or any other blemish, but holy and blameless" (Ephesians 5:27). A stain would indicate a soiled garment (contaminated life), while wrinkles might come from sitting or lying down (idleness)—or perhaps a Church that is acting old and tired. The wedding garment that Christ provides is to be kept spot and wrinkle free by living clean and staying active. If we are to be ready for the coming Bridegroom there are some changes in store for us.

Christ will not leave that work solely to the ingenuity of people. He will engineer circumstances as He sees fit to bring His bride into conformity with His plans. How we react to them is the key to the condition of our spiritual health.

This is and will continue to be a time of testing for us. Keeping bitterness out of the heart through these times is essential if we are to be "accounted worthy to escape all these things that shall come to pass, and to stand before the Son of man" (Luke 21:36b, KJV).

15

Summary

Every part of life involves relationships. All relationships are important to God because His Kingdom on earth is expressed through relationships. First between Him and His people, then among His people to each other, and then between His people and those in the world to whom the gospel is being proclaimed.

As we grow in the love of the Lord, our relationships will reflect the life of submission that our Lord demonstrated, and which the Holy Spirit nurtures in us through His love. In the final sense, submission is love in work shoes.

Jesus taught love throughout His earthly ministry. He said, "If you love me, you will obey what I command" (John 14:15). He then said, "My command is this: Love each other as I have loved you" (John 15:12). Our Lord's redeeming, all encompassing, love is clear in all that is recorded of Him. We receive from Him and pass it on to others.

Jesus set an example of how to please the Father and taught His followers to do the same. He drew strength from communion with His Father through frequent prayers. In that, He is our example as well. If we're to have the power of the Holy Spirit made available to us, we, too, must be people of prayer.

Jesus established His authority as head of His church through demonstration of the Holy Spirit's power, which He had received at the beginning of His ministry (Luke 3:22). After the resurrection, Jesus ascended to heaven and sent the Holy Spirit to His disciples so they could carry on the work of His Church in that same power.

That's what the day of Pentecost was all about. The disciples in the upper room anticipated and welcomed the Holy Spirit's coming while they waited and prayed in one accord. The Spirit still empowers those who receive Him today, and reveals Jesus Christ to them.

The Holy Spirit is easily grieved and leaves a church ("Ichabod"—1 Samuel 4:21) when there is disharmony among believers. The secret to harmony is love. The secret to the easy flow of love is mutual trust and respect, out of which submission comes naturally as each one gives preference to the other. Add to that, responsibility and accountability in all that is done and you have the makings of a good atmosphere for the Holy Spirit to remain and empower the church.

> Do nothing out of selfish ambition or vain conceit, but in humility consider others better than yourselves.
>
> Each of you should look not only to your own interests, but also to the interests of others.
>
> Your attitude should be the same as that of Christ Jesus:

Who, being in very nature God, did not consider equality with God something to be grasped,

but made himself nothing, taking the very nature of a servant, being made in human likeness.

And being found in appearance as a man, he humbled himself and became obedient to death—even death on a cross!　　　　(Philippians 2:3-8)

If you really desire to be a good servant of the Lord Jesus, the Holy Spirit will enable you to do these things as you put Christ and others first and put to death the old selfish nature. We must pray, not only for each other, but together, drawing strength from one another for re-enforcement. Just as love is a choice, so is selfishness and fear. Love is from God. Selfishness and fear come from the kingdom of darkness. Choose which you will serve.

"But if serving the LORD seems undesirable to you, then choose for yourselves this day whom you will serve, . . . But as for me and my household, we will serve the LORD."　　　　(Joshua 24:15)

In the words of M. Scott Peck, "There are only two states of being: submission to God and goodness or the refusal to submit to anything beyond one's own will—which refusal automatically enslaves one to the forces of evil. We must ultimately belong to either God or the devil. This paradox was, of course, expressed by Christ when He said, 'Whosoever will save his life shall lose it. And whosoever shall lose his life for my sake

185

shall find it' (Matthew 10:39). As C. S. Lewis put it, 'There is no neutral ground in the universe: every square inch, every split second is claimed by God and counter-claimed by Satan.'"[1]

The choices we make are truly a matter of life or death.

Christ Jesus wants to be the Lord of our choices.

He must be—or we have chosen death.

[1]*People of The Lie* by M. Scott Peck, MD, (© Copyrighted 1983, Simon & Schuster, NY).